Tea with Elisabeth

Tributes to Hospice Pioneer Dr. Elisabeth Kübler-Ross

Muhammad Ali • Sarah Ferguson, Duchess of York • Stephen Levine
Raymond Moody • Bernie Siegel • J. Donald Schumacher • Marianne Williamson
Melina Kanakaredes • Doreen Virtue • Gerald Jampolsky and Diane Cirincion
Barbara Brennan • Balfour M. Mount • Gladys T. McGarey • Dame Cicely Saunders
Robert T. McCall • Florence Wald • Barbara Marx Hubbard • Mwalimu Imara
Cathleen Fanslow-Brunjes • Stefan Haupt • Caroline Myss • Hetty Rodenburg
Johanna M. Treichler • C. Norman Shealy • John G. Rogers • Susanne Schaup
Rita Ward • Gregg M. Furth • D. Brookes Cowan • Ken Ross • Barbara Rothweiler
Sylvia and Emma Rothweiler • Eva Kübler-Bacher • Susan Elisabeth Bacher
Rick Hurst • Joan Halifax Roshi • Anneloes Eterman • Cheryl Shohan
Joanne Cacciatore • Amy Kuebelbeck • Carol Kearns • Hervé Mignot
Robert Singleton • Tom Hockemeyer • Ryoko Dozono • Elayne Reyna
Juan Francisco "Frank" Aráuz • Bette Croce • Rose Winters
Hope Sacharoff • Fern Stewart Welch

Executive Editor: Fern Stewart Welch
Associate Editor: Rose Winters
Photography Editor: Ken Ross

Published by Quality of Life Publishing Co.

PO Box 112050
Naples, Florida 34108-1929

Quality of Life Publishing Co. is an independent publisher inspired by the compassionate work of Dr. Elisabeth Kübler-Ross and dedicated to furthering the ideals of hospice care. For information about our physician education newsletters and growing family of gentle grief support and other uplifting books, visit www.QoLpublishing.com or call toll free 1-877-513-0099.

ISBN: 978-0-9816219-9-9

First Printing. Printed in the United States of America.

Library of Congress Control Number: 2009925338

The invitation to once again "take tea" with Elisabeth through the pages of this book was graciously accepted by 51 delighted guests.
The authors offered their commentaries and personal memories as gifts.
We dedicate Tea with Elisabeth *to each of them.*
We were deeply touched by their shared memories of Elisabeth, and also blessed, honored, and inspired by their generosity of spirit. We thank them from the bottom of our hearts.

Acknowledgments

We acknowledge the inspiration that brought the three of us together on a project that was meant to be. We know this book simply could not have happened without the commitment, passion, and unique capabilities of each individual.

We were extremely fortunate to have the wise counsel and guidance of Boyé Lafayette De Mente, a noted author of 50 books on the languages and cultures of Asia, and Rebecca Mong, a veteran writer and editor. They reviewed the manuscript at progressive stages and were generous with their input and advice, as well as unwavering in their wholehearted support of the importance of this project.

We are grateful for the expert guidance and counsel of our agent, Barbara Hogenson, who took our shared vision and made it a reality. Her belief in the project and in us was invaluable.

To Karla Wheeler, Dianne Gray, Kelly Brachle, and everyone at Quality of Life Publishing Company: Our heart's desire was to share the full story of Elisabeth's loving and selfless service to humanity. The world needs heroes more than ever right now, and *Tea with Elisabeth* will inspire many others to step forward to answer destiny's call. Our partnership with such a committed, passionate, and talented team made the journey pure pleasure.

We acknowledge and salute all the caring physicians, nurses, aides, social workers, chaplains, hospice workers and volunteers, the unsung heroes in end-of-life care, who embraced Elisabeth and her evolutionary work and helped bring death and dying into the light of compassion and reason.

Our deepest appreciation is reserved for the 51 wonderful contributors whose loving gifts to Elisabeth exceeded our highest expectations. Thank you, thank you, and thank you.

— *Fern Stewart Welch, Rose Winters, and Ken Ross*

Introduction

By Fern Stewart Welch

The idea for this book came to me in full form as I was writing a tribute for the memorial service following the death of Elisabeth Kübler-Ross. It was immediately obvious that such a project would need the collaboration of Kenneth Ross, Elisabeth's son, and Rose Winters, a friend of Elisabeth's who had loved and helped her through the last years of her life. They enthusiastically joined with me in bringing the project to life.

At first we planned an elegant coffee-table book with impressive color photographs and equally impressive commentaries from the world's luminaries. But as responses to the request letters began to come in, we knew that forces other than our own were at work, and the book was taking on a life of its own.

Virtually all of the responses we received were from people around the world who had met and worked with Elisabeth — not from kings and queens or the rich and famous we first thought might contribute to the book because of the work she had done on behalf of humanity. The commentaries and memories from her friends, co-workers, and collaborators brought added awareness of the magnitude of the contribution she made to the lives of millions of people around the world.

We already knew that she almost single-handedly brought death and dying out of the Dark Ages and into the light of reason and compassion, allowing individuals to die with dignity surrounded by loved ones. We also knew that she was a catalyst for the inception of patients' rights in America. What we couldn't know back then was that the effect of her revolutionary work would be ongoing. In the years following her death, her influence continues in the strong international movement seeking greater awareness of how to deal with long-term illnesses and the death process itself.

Even those of us who were the closest to Elisabeth began to gain new insights into the life and persona of this incredible woman through the eyes and experiences of each contributor.

We were deeply moved by the realization that even when the time spent with Elisabeth was extremely brief, the impact was powerfully and indelibly etched in the minds of those she had touched directly during her remarkable life. We began to understand that these commentaries would be the true heart and value of the book *Tea with Elisabeth*.

We also learned that Elisabeth's impact wasn't limited to her patients and those who came from all over the world for help. It was also experienced by anyone near her who was open to growing, changing, and stepping forward to fulfill their own unique life mission.

Many leaders in hospice and palliative care, as well as allied fields, who are now nationally known (some are bestselling authors) were delighted and eager to acknowledge their encounters with Elisabeth and explain how she changed their lives.

It became a fascinating daily adventure to read the personal memories and see how creative the universe can be in bringing souls who were to meet and work with Elisabeth into her presence. We were brought to tears most often when reading the behind-the-scene remembrances that provided a deeper insight into the solitary path that Elisabeth walked.

It was obvious that in the process of following her destiny, Elisabeth was to sacrifice much. She was divorced from her beloved husband,

Manny, and was able to be with her adored children only on rare occasions. She experienced dark times when she faced the loneliness of her chosen path, global criticism and microscopic scrutiny, as well as supernatural happenings that would have undone those of us who are of lesser mettle.

As is the case with similar souls who are driven to meet a great destiny, whoever emerges from the ranks to help the cause becomes a handmaiden. It is a blessing that there were some along the way who realized that Elisabeth and her message were a gift to humanity and were able to love her unconditionally.

So much of Elisabeth's inner life was being brought to light by the commentaries, ushering in a flood of my own memories. Elisabeth was extremely fond of the ritual of taking tea, and it was synonymous with a visit with her. You were hardly inside the door before she asked you or someone else to put on the kettle. It was her way of immediately bonding and sharing in an extremely disconnected world. This innate ability to create deep communion with individuals translated easily to a thousand spellbound participants at her lectures, and eventually to a global community of millions who were united by the clarity of her message and the courage and commitment to serving humanity.

I also recalled a time when I had asked Elisabeth to join with a group of my female friends for an impromptu afternoon tea on the desert. It was springtime and acres of riotous color blanketed the desert floor. She was partially wheelchair-bound and readily accepted the invitation for a change of venue.

We picked her up in a mini-van that would accommodate her wheelchair. On a lovely, elevated spot that allowed us a panoramic view of the area, we set up the draped table, and then busied ourselves picking wildflowers for a bouquet and arranging the sweets and delicacies that Elisabeth loved.

I vaguely noticed that Elisabeth was uncommonly quiet and within, but I was so caught up in the joy of bringing us together and the glorious day, that I didn't think about it again until much later.

After we situated her back in her cozy corner at home and my friends trooped out to the waiting van, I lingered a few minutes. She looked at me with what I read as a mixture of surprise and awareness, and said, "I have never been alone with a group of women like that." At the time I truly didn't understand the depth of her comment.

Now I do. After reading the commentaries, I realize she had probably never been with a group of women in a totally informal social situation that had nothing to do with her life mission and who needed or wanted nothing from her.

The commentaries also confirmed an intuitive knowing I had held for a long time. I believed from my own experience with Elisabeth and those of other acquaintances that there was a natural response in Elisabeth to anyone who came into her presence. I sensed that she was capable of "reading" the essence of people she met through her own energy system.

She often said to me and others, "I can smell a phony baloney," and she meant it. I believe she knew immediately upon meeting people why they had come to her, what their soul mission was, and how she was to interact with them. Many times, of course, she had no soul mission with people who sought her out for their own selfish purposes. When that happened, Elisabeth — never one to hide her displeasure — would respond with a demeanor that said, "Get out of my face."

In my own experience with her, I think she recognized my sensitivities and my growing ability to speak up for myself. She reacted to me with great tenderness, love, and respect. I certainly related to author Cheryl Shohan's comment that when she spoke up for herself to Elisabeth, Elisabeth loved it.

In my very first meeting with Elisabeth I firmly — and rightfully — challenged something she said. We locked eyes and experienced a mutual respect and soul contact that never wavered in ten years. I promised myself that in all my dealings with her I would always tell her the truth even though she might not like it, but it would always be the truth, as far as I knew it.

We had many conversations about life, family, husbands, and particularly about our children and grandchildren. I was able to present some truths that I had learned from some of the mistakes I had made along the way. I never said do this or that, or preached, which was not my style. I just calmly and lovingly shared my experiences from the heart, and she listened.

At this time, almost five years after her death, I realize that through the passion and commitment I have experienced in compiling this book, I continue to be affected by our connection. As many of the authors in this book also affirm, there is no doubt that the rest of our lives will be indelibly marked by our association with Elisabeth.

I think she met each soul exactly where it was, and went from there. If you were open to living your dreams and following your destiny, she was there to support and help you. If you were content with where you were, that was okay, too. The only ironclad requirement that seemed to be unilateral and totally nonnegotiable with her was that people should be absolutely authentic.

Those who knew her will find that in reading this book, some of the puzzling aspects of her life will begin to fall into place. Those who didn't know her will discover the private side of Elisabeth through the memories of those who lived it with her, whether they were family, friends, associates, patients or someone who simply shared a brief encounter with her.

Tea with Elisabeth brings insight into a heroic life lived by an individual who was only human, and yet achieved a truly singular destiny. She was that rare human being with extraordinary gifts who accepted a mission that was greater than her own desires for the companionship and love that is is inherent in everyone.

Elisabeth had to draw on raw courage, absolute commitment, and dogged resolve in the face of extreme opposition and open hostility to do what she was called to do — often alone. She was frequently maligned and misunderstood, and yet she never gave up or gave in. She always knew innately that it wasn't about her. It was about the message.

As fame elevates a soul to international icon status, the individual is often known only by their public persona and in the process of being idolized and idealized, they are also often dehumanized. This was the case with Elisabeth, as she became known to millions as only "the death and dying lady."

She was so much more. We believe this comes through in the powerful, poignant, and inspirational stories told by those whose lives were touched by a small dynamo of a woman who became a global force for change, and yet who was so completely, wonderfully, beautifully, painfully human.

Contents

*"There is within each of us
a potential for goodness
beyond our imagining,
for giving which seeks no
reward, for listening without
judgment, for loving
unconditionally."*

— Elisabeth Kübler-Ross, M.D.

A Chance Encounter with Destiny

By Balfour M. Mount, O.C., O.Q., M.D., F.R.C.S.C.

One of the four acknowledged architects of the international hospice movement, Balfour Mount maintained a close friendship with Elisabeth for more than three decades. He sheds light on Elisabeth's "rock-star" status, and how she was "perpetually in the center of a maelstrom of controversy."

The news of Elisabeth's death on August 24, 2004, filled me with a sense of loss and gratitude, not to mention a host of memories. Few people have played as significant a role in my life. I was instantly transported back to my first encounter with Elisabeth Kübler-Ross. It was in the early 1970s during her first lecture at McGill University in Montreal, Canada. I had not yet read her book *On Death and Dying* and attended that late afternoon Grand Rounds as the result of a chance comment by a colleague. I can see Elisabeth's eyes twinkle and hear her comment, "Naturally! Nothing ever happens by chance!"

The scene was aberrant, if not bizarre. The amphitheatre was packed, all 350 seats taken. Senior colleagues sat two abreast on each of the stairs; a throng of cross-legged students packed together on the floor around a table that served as an impromptu throne for our casually perched, visiting professor.

Arriving late, I managed to shoehorn my way into the crowd at the back of the auditorium. I can still see the eminent neurologist Francis McNaughton — or "Saint Francis," as he was commonly called — one of McGill's icons of clinical competence and grace, balanced on his toes, straining to see from the third row of standees behind the uppermost row of seats. There was an air of great expectancy.

I had only recently been recruited by McGill to further develop the surgical subspecialty dealing with genitourinary cancers, but following this encounter with Elisabeth, I found myself at a life-transforming crossroads. Things evolved quickly. We studied the deficiencies in end-of-life care at our hospital. Reading *On Death and Dying* put me in touch with the groundbreaking work of Dame Cicely Saunders at St. Christopher's Hospice, London.

We subsequently designed a hospital-based "hospice equivalent" that involved a home care program, a consultation service, a specialized ward — the Palliative Care Unit — and a bereavement follow-up program, as well as research and teaching activities. We had two years to show that such an innovation was worthwhile.

During the 1975-76 Royal Victoria Hospital Palliative Care Service pilot project, Elisabeth was a constant mentor, a frequent visitor, and a source of unending encouragement. Our experiment in end-of-life care was a great success. The result was the first comprehensive Palliative Care Program — a name that allowed us, in our francophone province, to avoid the pejorative connotations associated with *"les hospices"* in France. Within 18 months we were able to show that the hospice model pioneered by Dame Cicely could be duplicated within an academic teaching hospital. Elisabeth was delighted!

Those were heady days. Our patients became our teachers. The term "interdisciplinary team" took on a new egalitarian meaning. The difference between disease and illness became glaringly clear, as did the need for integrated whole-person care. Over the months following my "chance" encounter with Elisabeth, my surgical practice, chemotherapy clinic, and research laboratory were taken over by others. I turned my attention to the needs of the dying on a full-time basis.

In October 1976, Elisabeth was a featured speaker at McGill's first International Congress on the Care of the Terminally Ill. Her sage contributions to the volatile discussions during that landmark meeting were noteworthy. She had an uncanny ability to put her finger on the issue, to assess the biases of the combatants, and to offer insightful, healing observations.

Later that same night, after she returned home, I received a phone call from her in Chicago. I warmed at the sound of that familiar voice, but her message was short and to the point. "Bal," she intoned, "I have only two things to say. First, it was a wonderful conference, and second, give up your insecurity. You don't need it!" Now there's a friend!

We remained in touch, and I could always count on her. As time passed, Elisabeth became a celebrity of rock-star proportions, and she found herself perpetually at the center of a maelstrom of controversy.

Lionized by some, demonized by others, Elisabeth evoked a feeding frenzy! Her integrity was harshly questioned. Had she plagiarized the work of others? Did she believe that the end always justified the means — any means? Did she knowingly acquiesce in suspect activities in the belief that deluded, vulnerable people once liberated from all constraints would be set free? Were her spooks and spirit guides figments of an overactive imagination, merely a good yarn, or the product of flamboyant spiritual openness? Was she vilified, tormented, and terrorized by her house being burned down because she walked a martyr's path of unwelcome honesty, or did she unconsciously incite hostility born in envy or fear? Did her highly public proclamations supporting, then decrying, the spiritual life, issue from a need to be in the spotlight?

Maybe our insatiable need for heroes leaves us resentful when we encounter their humanity and thus are confronted with our own deepest uncertainties and questions.

As for me, I will remember Elisabeth for her openness, generosity of spirit, and incomparable listening skills. And what a storyteller! No one can forget that mesmerizing "Switzer-Germanglish" twang; her ability to create a sense of intimacy with an audience numbering in the hundreds or even thousands; her sensitivity in interviewing an anguished stranger, only to leave all present more in touch with their own personal journey.

Elisabeth was one of the truly great communicators of the 20th century. Her impact as a teacher has been global in scope. She shed light on how we come to terms with loss and impending death and gave voice to those disenfranchised by their experiences "at the edge of being."

Elisabeth was a courageous pilgrim whose path has led to health-care reform, existential questioning, and relief of suffering in countries around the world. We were enriched by her presence. She left this world a much better place and my life immeasurably enriched.

I remember waiting for her after one of her talks. The waiting seemed endless. She told me later, "You know, Bal, the personal chats with people in need that follow the talk are the most important part." How different from the egocentric response of some acclaimed gurus!

Elisabeth's generosity was endless. What a blessing she was! What a refreshing character! What a dear and faithful friend!

Dr. Balfour Mount became founding director of the Royal Victoria Hospital Palliative Care Service in Montreal, Canada, in 1975. Since 1976 he has been chairperson of McGill University's biennial International Congresses on Care of the Terminally Ill. He has authored more than 140 publications, and participated in the production of 25 teaching films and audiotapes on oncology and palliative care.

The Light within Elisabeth

By Gladys T. McGarey, M.D., M.D.(H)

As one of Elisabeth's personal physicians during the last decade of
her life, Dr. McGarey was able to sift through all the symptoms and
see with objectivity and tenderness the true essence of
Elisabeth Kübler-Ross.

I don't believe there is a person anywhere in the world who hasn't
been touched in some way by the work of Elisabeth Kübler-
Ross and blessed by her very being-ness. She has changed the face of
medicine, as well as the face of human acceptance of life itself.

Elisabeth understood that life is a passage with a beginning and an
end, and that it was time for humanity to face the end of life with as
much awareness, dignity, and love as that accorded to birth. Bringing
this truth to the world became her life mission.

It has been a true gift to count her as a friend for more than 30
years. When we first met on the speaking platform in the 1970s, it
was as if we brought together the circle of life. I spoke about birth.

She covered death and dying. There were other similarities also. We had become physicians when women were greatly discouraged in this profession. We were pioneers and spokespersons in areas that were far from acceptable to the medical establishment. I was in holistic-alternative medicine, and Elisabeth was a global force pushing against the centuries-old taboos that prevented talking openly about death and dying.

The path she would travel to benefit humanity was evident at an early age. She was born in Zurich, Switzerland, on July 8, 1926, the first of a set of triplets and at two pounds, the smallest. She came in filled with the fighting spirit that had been a signature trait all her life. As a youngster she was always battling for the underdog.

At the age of 13, she heard on the radio in Switzerland that Germany had invaded Poland. She was so moved by the tragedy she affirmed to her parents: "I vow that unless I die, and no matter what else happens, I will come to help the Polish people as soon as I can." She would fulfill that vow at the tender age of 19. In 1946 as a member of the International Volunteer Service for Peace, she received the call to go to Poland. She was headquartered at a hospital where she not only cooked for 45 volunteers, but also assisted two female physicians who comprised the hospital staff.

Just before Elisabeth left this assignment, a woman came to the hospital with a baby who was dying of typhoid. The mother had walked two days to get there. Elisabeth knew they had nothing on site that would help the baby. But 20 miles away was a larger hospital, so she and this woman walked all night. At first, the hospital physician told them that nothing could be done, but Elisabeth convinced him to take the baby anyway. After 12 days, the mother returned to pick up her healthy baby. She gave Elisabeth a handkerchief full of her beloved Polish soil, which Elisabeth always kept near her.

Elisabeth subsequently became a psychiatrist, author, and lecturer, and as a force of nature, she changed the way the world thinks about death and dying with her universal message.

The stories of Elisabeth's incredible capacity for human caring and compassion are legendary. They are told again and again whenever people, who have been touched by her life and work, write about her or gather to speak about her.

She came back into my life on a more intimate basis in 1995. Several strokes had caused her son, Ken, to bring her to Scottsdale, Arizona, to recuperate. It was a privilege to become one of her personal physicians.

Here we were in the sunset of our lives, two veterans of many battles, now able to share and to appreciate the changes that had been wrought because we were called to pick up the torch and carry it forward.

Shortly after moving to Arizona, Elisabeth fractured her hip and was pretty much immobilized. That was a huge challenge to this tiny dynamo of a woman. She was used to helping others, not being helped. It was a very difficult time for Elisabeth.

She had created a place for herself in the pristine Arizona desert, replete with a teepee in her front yard, a totem pole that she brought from her headquarters in Virginia, and the flag of Switzerland waving proudly from the roof of the house. Her body may have been compromised, but not her mind. She continued writing books and providing tea, empathy, compassion, and caring for the thousands of visitors from around the world.

One of the things I loved and appreciated about Elisabeth was her unwavering insistence on authenticity and truth. One of her signature statements was, "That's not phony baloney," and this was her highest compliment. This was the core of Elisabeth.

Since she was one of the most famous women in the world, the media covered her struggles with the death process in such detail that many may have wondered if this was the incredible soul who had helped so many millions deal with death and dying. Yes, this was Elisabeth, the shoot-from-the-lip feisty human being who was coming to grips with her own mortality and just telling it like it was at that moment — and some of those moments were uncomfortable and totally unacceptable to her. I believe that in her own inimitable way, she was eventually able to come to peace with life and death.

One of her quotes that I hold dear to my heart is: "People are like stained-glass windows. They sparkle and shine when the sun is out, but when the darkness sets in their true beauty is revealed only if there is a light from within."

Elisabeth truly had this light within, and it not only attracted people to her, it evoked an outpouring of love on an individual and global scale that is all too rare. She was one of the great souls of the world, and I am better for having known her.

Dr. Gladys McGarey was a family physician for more than 50 years. She is internationally known for her pioneering work in holistic medicine, natural birthing, and the physician-patient partnership. She is the author of two books, *The Physician within You* and *Born to Live*. Dr. McGarey recently completed a humanitarian mission in Afghanistan under the auspices of a non-profit foundation — Future Generations — working with a female physician to bring healthcare to women and children in rural areas.

Champion of Life

By Muhammad Ali

Muhammad Ali is considered the best boxer of all time. He recognized in Elisabeth a fighter with a similar ability to "float like a butterfly and sting like a bee."

Peace is a concept that will always be associated with Elisabeth; it seemed to radiate from her as if from an angel. I've never met anyone as full of energy or as independent as Elisabeth, who remained humble and remarkably comfortable with herself all at the same time. Her ability to share this unique understanding of peace and comfort — especially during life's challenging moments — was but one of many things that made her special.

Knowing Elisabeth and having the opportunity to spend time with her continues to be an important and memorable experience for me. People tell me that she was one of my biggest fans, and the truth is I was one of hers. The good work she so selflessly did for people, especially for children, is inspirational to me and to so many others. Her life and work are great examples of how to affect positive change in the world, while remaining honest and true to one's beliefs.

Elisabeth used to say that true beauty is revealed only if there is a light from within, and I believe this simple philosophy is perhaps the most powerful awareness we can achieve. She taught us that self-realization is an important part of understanding the meaning of life, as well as our individual lives. It is not coincidence, then, that the woman who taught us so much about death and dying as a process was truly the greatest champion of life.

One of my favorite quotes by Elisabeth has to do with the purpose of life, a topic that I think about often: "Learn to get in touch with the silence within you and know that everything in this life has a purpose." I celebrate this truth in her memory.

Muhammad Ali has written a spiritual autobiography, *The Soul of a Butterfly*. He and his wife, Lonnie, work together to further tolerance and understanding of all people around the world. Secretary General Kofi Annan acknowledged his international work by naming him a United Nations Messenger of Peace. His inspirational work is being furthered through the Muhammad Ali Museum and Education Center in Louisville, Kentucky.

A Salute to Our Common Humanity

By Dame Cicely Saunders, O.M., D.B.E., F.R.C.P., F.R.C.N.

Dame Cicely Saunders is the acknowledged founder of the international hospice movement, and had a high regard for Elisabeth's work.

I first met Elisabeth Kübler-Ross in 1966 when I was a visiting lecturer on Care of the Dying at Yale University's School of Nursing. During my time there, Elisabeth came to a seminar arranged by the then-dean, Florence Wald.

The attendees also included Dr. Colin Murray Parkes, a social psychiatrist from London's Tavistock Centre for Human Relations, with whom I had been in contact concerning his work on bereavement. He was working with John Bowlby, Psy.D., who had identified the three stages of separation anxiety in children. Dr. Parkes presented Dr. Bowlby's concept of the stages of grief. It is likely that this could have had an influence on Elisabeth's ground-breaking theory of the stages of dying, which was to have such an impact, particularly in the

United States, following publication of her book *On Death and Dying* in 1969. Its subsequent influence worldwide and the lectures she gave with such indefatigable zeal can scarcely be overestimated.

At that seminar, I presented my description of total pain, in which I described the patient's whole experience as including physical, emotional, social (or family), and spiritual components. This concept, first presented in 1964, was based on my seven-year Fellowship (1958-65) and research on The Nature and Management of Terminal Pain. Dr. Parkes pointed out over dinner with Elisabeth and me that we were working in different time scales: Elisabeth in hours and me in weeks. Then he added, "My research group of widows took two years to reach the state of acceptance we were all describing."

Sharing a platform with Elisabeth several times over the following few years, I was deeply impressed by the way her charismatic, inspirational lectures enabled both professional and lay publics to understand that death and dying could be faced and discussed without fear, as well as giving to people at the end of their lives a chance to find personal growth and family reconciliation. Her books became not only an introduction to fresh ideas for nurses, social workers, psychiatrists (and later physicians) — bringing them to the bedside with a new confidence — they also became bestsellers that instigated a remarkable change in public attitudes.

Fundamental social change does not happen until society is prepared for it. Elisabeth's work was instrumental in preparing the world stage to accept such a change. The subsequent development of hospice care in the United States was led initially by Florence Wald. She resigned as dean of nursing at Yale to carry out a series of studies of dying patients and their experiences at the end of life. By 1974, after spending a sabbatical at St. Christopher's Hospice in London, she returned to the U.S., and set up a home care team in Connecticut. By having no back-up beds at the hospital in New Haven, Connecticut, she demonstrated that the new teaching could be transferred to care in a patient's home.

Elisabeth's pioneering studies and enthusiasm were largely responsible for capturing people's interest and motivating them to become part of this effort. Elisabeth challenged the established teaching that forbade personal involvement with patients. My work at St. Joseph's and later St. Christopher's Hospices contradicted textbook teaching about the dangers of adequate and timely doses of opioids for end-of-life pain.

By the time St. Christopher's Hospice opened for in-patient care in 1967 (with home care started in1969), Elisabeth and I had written and lectured widely on the holistic approach to end-of-life care. We had also demonstrated that the regular giving of opioids, based on patient need, could relieve pain while enabling the patient to remain alert and able to try to fulfill their final aspirations without problems of tolerance or addiction. Thus, the ground was laid for the subsequent development of clinical and psychological sophistication in this area.

When Elisabeth's book *On Death and Dying* was translated into many languages, this system became available to people of different cultures and resources who wished to enter this rewarding field of medicine and human endeavour.

Elisabeth's remarkable capacity to inspire public acceptance and the development of hospice and later palliative care could be likened to two blades of a pair of scissors, able together to cut patient bonds of isolation and pain. Our work has been complementary, as we have built on the insights of our predecessors.

To the end of her well-lived life, Elisabeth certainly gave of herself unstintingly, and countless people owe her an immense debt. She showed how her direct approach could be translated worldwide. The stories and recordings of her patients have led people of all professions involved with the needs of the dying to match science with personal concern.

Others will find new ways to tackle the many unsolved problems that remain in psychological understanding and symptom control. Those currently working in the field continue to develop the knowledge that has spread so quickly in the last few decades. It is from the dying themselves that we learn about death. We must not forget to listen to our patients and their families, and give them their true place in society.

Elisabeth's work, coupled with all the continuing effort carried out by hospice teams taking place day-by-day worldwide, is a salute to our common humanity. It is a legacy that will remain.

Dame Cicely Saunders died in 2005, shortly after she wrote the above essay. She founded St. Christopher's Hospice in London in 1967. It was the world's first research and teaching hospice linked with clinical care, and also a pioneer in the field of palliative medicine. She received many honors and awards for her numerous life achievements, including the Order of Merit, the highest honor bestowed by Her Majesty, the Queen of England.

With Heart, Soul, and Humour

By Sarah Ferguson, Duchess of York

When touched by personal grief, the Duchess of York found in
Elisabeth the perfect healing combination of
compassion, comfort, and humour.

I first met Elisabeth in 1995, and during that first meeting I was
struck by her extraordinary energy and zest for life. Here was a
woman who dealt with the most difficult of human situations, and I
was overwhelmed by her optimism, her kindness, and her wonderful
sense of humour.

I learnt so much from Elisabeth, and when I lost anyone dear to me,
I would always heed her words of comfort and support. To lose a loved
one is the most traumatic and devastating experience, and however prepared you are for the eventuality, death still has a colossal impact on
those who are left behind.

Elisabeth has done so much for so many bereaved people all over the
world, and I admire her work tremendously. She has helped people in

great pain, and I believe that she had a true gift. She has enabled people to come to terms with the wide range of emotions associated with death, such as anger and regret.

I once asked Elisabeth, "Can I send you anything from London?" and she replied, "I would love some dark chocolate from Switzerland and some menthol cigarettes from Dunhill. They don't let me smoke, but perhaps you could sneak them in for me!" She had such a light-hearted, huge sense of humour.

My grandmother always said that God gave us a pure heart, a pure soul, and humour. She said that God gave us these attributes so that we could use them.

I will always remember Elisabeth with great affection and salute her for her tremendous hard work and compassion. She was an all-rounded, magical example of a shining star.

Sarah Ferguson, the Duchess of York, is the single mother of two daughters, Princesses Beatrice and Eugenie. A bestselling author, she has written almost two dozen books on a variety of subjects, including diet, nutrition, and self-improvement. She has written a series of children's books, several historical books, and three autobiographical books: *My Story, A Guard Within,* and *What I Know Now: Lessons Learned the Hard Way.* She is also the founder of two charitable organizations that focus on the urgent needs of children.

Astronaut of Inner Space

By Robert T. McCall

NASA artist Robert McCall probed the far reaches of outer space with his paintings to bring the future to light. He recognized a fellow explorer in Elisabeth, who plumbed the depths of inner space.

Every now and then, a great personality appears on earth with powerful intellectual and spiritual insight that propels humankind to new levels of understanding.

Elisabeth Kübler-Ross was just such a person, a pioneer who led the human spirit to new horizons. She brought death into the light of fresh comprehension, calming our fears, and bringing new knowledge about the intricate patterns of the dying process.

At the same time that our nation's space program and the astronauts were seeking new knowledge of the universe and venturing into outer space, she was exploring the inner space of the human condition.

19

Elisabeth Kübler-Ross and the five stages of dying that she recognized and established have become a permanent part of the dying process for many in the Western world. These five stages give us a great road map for living as well as dying. Not only are these steps a comforting way to address our natural fear, but there is a fundamental truth about them: They stabilize us and present to us a gentler way to approach this necessary end that comes to us all.

She was an important force in creating the hospice program. This is one of the most significant additions to the manner in which we interact with those who are facing this last great adventure. Now there is an understanding as to how we may approach the end of life with equanimity, grace, and a calm that transcends our natural fears.

We are grateful that she was among us, bringing her gentle genius to serve and ease our way.

Robert McCall became one of a select group of artists chosen by NASA to document the United States space program. He has completed murals for Disney's EPCOT Center, Edwards Air Force Base, Johnson Space Center, and the Air Force Academy. His work is prominently displayed in the Pentagon, the Smithsonian Air and Space Museums, as well as in many distinguished private collections. His conceptual art for the film *2001: A Space Odyssey* has become a modern classic.

Sharing a Passion for Chocolate and Conversation

By Melina Kanakaredes

The star of the television show *CSI: New York* shares her salad days
and the joy of finding friends who became family in the
Big Apple.

In 1989 I moved to New York to further my acting career. Within a week I had arranged for temporary housing, gotten a weekend job as a waitress, and was doing some print modeling.

They used to call it "go sees," when you took your portfolio to a photographer in the hope of getting modeling jobs. I always tried to be sure the addresses were in good neighborhoods, and this particular one was on Madison Avenue. The photographer was Ken Ross. As he looked at my portfolio, I was admiring his beautiful apartment and noticed he had a large collection of books, especially books by Elisabeth Kübler-Ross.

I told him I loved her books, and as a psychology minor in college, I was very familiar with her work. He said, "She is my mother." We clicked immediately, and after a lengthy conversation I found myself sharing my current situation. Everything tumbled out: how I had just connected with a weekend job waitressing, needed a place to stay because my housing situation was shaky, and that I didn't want to go home.

He told me he was leaving for Africa the next morning on a photo shoot and offered me his apartment for the month he would be gone. I could hardly believe his generosity. I was overwhelmed and tried to decline, but he insisted that I was a nice Greek girl from Ohio and it would be all right.

While he was gone, Elisabeth telephoned to talk to Ken. She told me she was sorry to have missed him, and almost in the same breath asked, "Who are you?" I told her I was Melina, and she remembered Ken mentioning that I would be staying in his apartment. We exchanged pleasantries, including the fact that we were looking forward to meeting each other.

When Ken returned, our friendship continued. After about three months, Elisabeth came to New York to give a speech. Naturally, I was very nervous about our first meeting, as I thought she would be analyzing me. I knew she would be quite curious about my friendship with her son.

So I took the opportunity to attend one of her lectures and was stunned by the connection she had with an audience. They were spellbound. You could have heard a pin drop during her presentation, which was filled with humor, light, love, and universal truths. It was also obvious that the audience was somehow changed by this encounter, and I thought they were better for having been in her presence.

Within the first ten minutes after meeting her, she dubbed me "the kissy one," explaining that people who have a lot of affection to give need a lot of affection.

I called her *Mutti,* as did Ken; I think it is Swiss-German for mother. My place in the family as a dear friend was assured and continues to this day. Ken and I visited her wherever she was living, including Virginia and Arizona.

One of the most incredible aspects I noticed immediately about Elisabeth was the dichotomy between the public person, the one who traveled the world and touched millions of lives, and the private Elisabeth. It didn't matter that she was driven in her passion to bring a needed message to the world. She was also equally a loving mother, friend, and a wonderful homemaker. She had "put up" the most fantastic collection of preserves that I had ever seen. She loved her family. No matter what else was going on in her life, she thought of them.

The first dinner she served me included a traditional Swiss dish. She heated a large rock, on which was melted Swiss cheese, and the melted cheese was served over a baked potato.

One of my fondest memories of Elisabeth is of her care packages. Once Ken received what I considered a lifetime supply of cheese, and it smelled like it had taken a lifetime to arrive. Another time Ken drove a great distance to pick up an enormous amethyst crystal formation that she had bought for him. No matter the extreme demands on her time and life, she always thought of family.

While the world knew her as the death and dying lady, she was about love, life, and living to the fullest. She was about joy and laughter, and eating a lot of chocolate.

This was something else we shared in common. My family is in the chocolate business. When my grandfather came to this country from Greece, all he knew how to do was make chocolate. My uncles carry on this tradition to this day in their chocolate factory. They make hand-dipped chocolates with no preservatives. This shared passion for chocolate and conversation spanned our entire relationship.

I am so blessed to have known Elisabeth and to have spent time with her. Each time I think I have heard all the stories about her, someone will tell me something else about her that adds to the scope of her love and compassion.

She was so wonderfully nonjudgmental. Her love of people in general was exceeded only by her obsessive love and acceptance of children. She told me often of the great strength of children, and how those who were dying had such inner strength that they were able to help their grieving parents. When she interacted with children, she was transported to another plane.

When I was pregnant with my first child, she told me that people tell you they change your life. She said they come in perfect, and we mess them up. I think of this often with my own children, and treat them differently because of this.

Elisabeth's dream was to have a center that would carry on her work, and where the elderly and children would be brought together to heal each other. I know my dear friend Ken is working to make this happen.

Melina Kanakaredes, currently starring in *CSI: New York,* was nominated for two Emmys for her former role on the daily television drama *The Guiding Light*. She also appeared in *NYPD Blue,* and in feature films such as *15 Minutes,* with Robert DeNiro and *The Long Kiss Goodnight,* with Geena Davis and Samuel L. Jackson.

Comrade in Arms

By *Florence Wald, M.N., M.S., F.A.A.N.*

Along with Elisabeth, Dr. Balfour Mount, and Dame Cicely Saunders,
Florence Wald is credited with initiating the hospice movement.

Tea with Elisabeth is an odd image for me to ponder. I see her
with a baseball cap on her head, a cigarette in one hand, and a
chocolate ice cream cone in the other. She might upset the tea tray in
making a point and ask (in her mellifluous Swiss accent), "Don't you
have coffee?" One always knew that what Elisabeth said was what she
meant.

When we first met at a conference at Yale University in the spring
of 1966, she was one of only a handful of caregivers drawn to dying
patients. She came from Chicago, and Cicely Saunders and Colin
Murray Parkes, also doctors, came from London. Elisabeth's first book,
On Death and Dying, would not be published for three years.

I still remember her timeless gesture: With one hand on her dia-
phragm and the other on her brow she said, "Use your gut, not your

head, when listening to patients." That resonated with me! We were teaching our nursing students to listen to what the patient says or does, make sure to hear, and then make sure of the patient's meaning before taking action. Here was Elisabeth, a doctor, saying that, too, unlike the doctors we were working with, who dissuaded nurses from encouraging patients and families to discuss or involve them in decisions of care. We were in a time when patients' rights were beginning to be recognized. Elisabeth led in that reform.

In the next 10 years, we would meet many times. The number of diverse people drawn to care for those facing terminal illness multiplied quickly, and they sought each other out in various parts of the United States and abroad. Ultimately, they fell into two groups, affectionately called the "doers" and the "feelies." Elisabeth was mentor of the feelies.

I became one of the "doers." Having heard Dame Cicely Saunders, founder of St. Christopher's Hospice in London, and later, having spent an all too short period of time giving care there, I knew working toward something between a hospital and home was the right avenue for me. I knew it needed to be a place where multiple kinds of suffering were tended by an interdisciplinary team, and where patients and families came first.

I knew how much I needed to learn to treat symptoms, help families be part of the process, design a setting, find financial support, and engage the community. I also kept in touch with Elisabeth during this time.

In the next two decades, the number of colleagues from many disciplines grew swiftly in both groups. Elisabeth was sought out as a speaker of larger and larger audiences. Her writing expanded in popular journals. While we "doers" were learning our craft and working within the medical establishment, Elisabeth was set free of it.

After her book *On Death and Dying* was published, the Chicago University Medical School found little value in her direct and clear patient encounter and uncluttered conceptual framework. Her faculty appointment ended. When the hospital setting, in which she talked with dying patients, would no longer support her practice, she knew it in her heart, and she had the conviction and strength to seek new avenues.

During a study of patients we conducted at Yale, Elisabeth interviewed one of the patients before a large professional audience. The resistance of the medical community to her approach was swept aside by the eagerness with which the public accepted it.

Clergy and nurses were the first to value her understanding and approach. They were the ones to whom patients turned when doctors failed to answer questions. Forums continued outside university centers.

On one hand, the "doers" and the "feelies" differed in focus and style, but a synergy developed. The "doers" took on the medical establishment and the governors of health policy to whittle out units of palliative care in hospitals. The talking came first and then the hospices multiplied fast. Meanwhile, Elisabeth's lectures, workshops, writings, and consultations yielded a host of caregivers with interpersonal skills. Nurses had the greatest need for changing conventional nursing practice that had distanced patients for so long. There was no better guide than Elisabeth in supporting and understanding the patient-caregiver bond.

Nurses who needed Elisabeth's teaching were largely responsible for creating what can best be called a free university for her. At first, they would arrange for a lecture hall and then publicize the gathering. Elisabeth first came to lecture, but soon weekend workshops became the norm.

Audiences became larger and more diverse — clergy, members of congregations, families of patients, and patients themselves. Sites became more distant and events more frequent, with Elisabeth spending more time in the air, with few opportunities for rest, family, good food, and relaxation.

A permanent site was found for Elisabeth in California in order to limit both the expense and the time involved in her extensive traveling. Her work and accomplishments had come at a price for her family. It had been virtually impossible for her to be even a part-time wife and mother. Society's need and demand for change were relentless, and the call from her heart and soul was such that she could not put it aside, even to save her marriage.

When I saw Elisabeth for the last time in January 2004, though she was 12 years younger than I, her small body was frail and I was struck with how she had aged. The gleam, however, was still in her eye. She spread out her arms and we hugged. It hurt to see her in a small, meager space, but it didn't seem to bother her. As always, people were what mattered to her!

Many have heard Elisabeth say that, as the scrawniest triplet, there was no room for her on her mother's lap. Now that "scrawny little triplet" has become a soaring eagle.

The late Florence Wald, former dean of Yale University's School of Nursing, joined with a surgeon, a pediatrician, and a chaplain in 1971 to form the first hospice facility in the U.S. She has published articles and book chapters on hospice care and the training of nurses, and was working to set up hospice units in American prisons until her death in 2008. Her many honors included being inducted into the National Women's Hall of Fame in 1998.

A Brief Encounter

By Barbara Marx Hubbard

The spiritual hypothesis raised in Barbara Marx Hubbard's
bestselling book *The Revelation: Our Crisis is a Birth* ignited
Elisabeth's incredible curiosity and imagination.

My first and only encounter with Elisabeth Kübler-Ross was when she called me after reading my book *The Revelation: Our Crisis is a Birth,* which is an evolutionary interpretation of the New Testament that portrays Christ in the future as the next stage of human evolution.

Elisabeth loved the book and began a dialogue with me about human possibilities, about how death itself may be a stage, and how we might actually learn to have continuity of consciousness through many bodies, finally becoming ever-evolving human beings.

I did not have the pleasure of being with her, except in spirit. I feel that her courage in helping us overcome the fear of death by seeing death as a passageway is actually "thinning the veil" between worlds, opening for us a far greater horizon for human development than we have known before.

Barbara Marx Hubbard is a futurist and lecturer who authored four books, including *The Revelation: Our Crisis is a Birth* and *Conscious Evolution: Awakening the Power of Our Social Potential*. Her name was placed in nomination for the vice presidency of the United States on the Democratic ticket in 1984. She is president of The Foundation for Conscious Evolution.

A Memory of New Birth

By Mwalimu Imara, D.Min.

During the final work on her soon-to-be classic *On Death and Dying,*
Elisabeth turned for support and counsel to her friend and
colleague, Mwalimu Imara, then a resident chaplain at
University of Chicago Hospitals.

Of the many memories I have of Elisabeth Kübler-Ross, I
remember most the evening we spent together when her
book *On Death and Dying* was completed. It was the evening she permitted me to see a glimpse of the ground out of which her challenging book emerged.

The death and dying movement in the United States and around the
world began with the publishing of Elisabeth's book in 1969. *On Death
and Dying* raised the awareness and consciousness of health professionals and lay people about the cruelty of our institutional way of
dying.

I remember well the night when this revolution of insight began. Elisabeth had received the galley proofs from her publisher, and she invited me to her house to help with the finishing touches. The quotes from Rabindranath Tagore's works that open each chapter had to be selected. Actually she had already made the selections, but she wanted company. She was finished with the last chapter of the book, but she was not quite satisfied with the ending, so some revision or rewriting was needed there. Then there was that chapter that was not yet included in the book: a chapter on life after death. Should she include it, or should she not? This had to be decided.

After supper my wife, Harriet, who has since changed her name to Saburi, was sitting in the living room talking to Manny, Elisabeth's husband. Elisabeth cleared the table in the small kitchen just off the living room, and we approached the manuscript. It was after nine o'clock.

While I read through parts of the manuscript for the first time, Elisabeth hesitantly selected the Tagore quotes, sharing each selection with me for my opinion as to its aptness. Of course, my opinion was more about approval than censure. She had spent many previous hours fitting those Tagore quotes to each chapter.

Elisabeth was excited about her book. The evening wore on and we were looking at the last chapter. We both thought that it said what Elisabeth had intended it to say, but she felt that it wasn't finished and we should write a final paragraph together to close it, and so we did. I know that this was her way of thanking me for my support of her seminar, and for keeping her company through the tedious, lonely task of putting the final touches on a manuscript. But now the decision about the life after death chapter had to be made.

We both had been collecting first-person experiences from people whose hearts had stopped and been resuscitated. We listened to surviving families talk about their visitations from long-dead family members. We listened to children during the last days or hours of life describe a friendly stranger who visited and talked with them. Death took on less of a closed-wall appearance and seemed more of a swinging door. But the resuscitation stories held more excitement because they were from people in our own ICUs, our own wards, and our own hospital. Therefore, the stories could be readily checked.

We could not believe that anyone reading these cases would not be convinced, as we were, that there was more we could learn about the boundary between life and death. Certainly we had enough material to convincingly capture the attention of the most ardent skeptic.

We had enough examples. The substance was there. So, should Elisabeth include in her book that chapter on life after death? I told Elisabeth that a Unitarian minister friend of mine, Rhys Williams, had submitted a book that had a similar chapter in it, but his book was rejected because he refused to eliminate it.

Elisabeth speculated that her publisher might think that they were being *avant garde* in publishing a book on death and dying. Of course, we didn't know that *On Death and Dying* would be an international bestseller. She made the decision not to include the chapter. If there is a rich idea lying about undeveloped, it will eventually surface. It did several years later with Raymond Moody's book *Life After Life,* for which Elisabeth wrote the foreword.

The book discussion being finished, Elisabeth leaned back in her kitchen chair and became quiet. I thought she was tired after working a full day and editing all evening. Manny and Saburi were asleep in the living room.

I asked Elisabeth how she first became interested in death and dying. She did not answer me directly. She deflected the conversation by asking if I would like a whiskey sour, because she was going to make one for herself. The blender crushed the ice and mixed the prepared powdered mix with the liquor. Elisabeth poured the drink into two glasses, commenting on our comatose spouses in the living room.

She sat down, lit her cigarette, and again sat in silence. She leaned back in her chair, flicking her ashes into the tray, and said, "It's a long story. It's my story. I want to tell you so you will understand why this work means so much to me."

For the next hour-and-a-half she poured out her personal history in a quiet, almost monotone speech. Though her voice was quiet, the pictures she painted with her matter-of-fact attitude shouted loudly in my imagination.

She started her story with how she joined a small volunteer group dedicated to rebuilding lives after the Second World War. She then spoke about struggling to help others as a premedical student in postwar Poland. She then spoke quietly of the horror of visiting Maidanek, a concentration camp, a few months after the liberation of its prisoners. This is where hundreds of thousands of Jews were gassed and burned in ovens. She described how in her mind she could still imagine the smell of rotting flesh although years had passed since the ovens did their work of horror. She described the boxcars with their obscene cargo of human hair, children's clothes, and baby shoes. She was then a young woman in her late teens.

The lasting artifacts of cruel war had etched on her spirit a commitment to love and to challenge cruelty wherever she saw it.

This was not the first time she had told the story. But maybe this was the first time that she told the story and heard it herself. She paused. Elisabeth didn't sob or cry but let out a deep sigh that seemed full of tears. That sigh had the signature of her soul on it.

So this is what this book means to her, I thought. It is her weapon that she would use to wage love against inhumanity, cruelty, and oppression. Then I understood the genesis of her command to love, and how it became the central driving force in her life. She had answered my question.

The Reverend Dr. Mwalimu Imara is professor emeritus of Human Values and Ethics at Morehouse School of Medicine in Atlanta, Georgia. He is a professional staff member of the Gestalt Institute of Cleveland, where he teaches Gestalt methods of counseling. Dr. Imara worked with Elisabeth from the beginning of the death and dying movement at the University of Chicago Hospitals.

Is There Life After Life?

By Raymond Moody, Ph.D., M.D.

The bestselling author of *Life After Life* remembers
his friendship with Elisabeth.

I had the pleasure of meeting Elisabeth in the autumn of 1975, in Atlanta. My book *Life After Life* was about to be released, and my publisher had sent her an advance copy, sensing that she might be interested. I was truly overwhelmed and honored when she volunteered to write the foreword. After that, our paths crossed from time to time at various conferences, and always we enjoyed being together.

People are always surprised when I say that Elisabeth and I hardly ever talked about death and dying or life after death.

She remained somewhat baffled that I continued to insist that near-death experiences are not scientific evidence of an afterlife, and indeed, that the afterlife is not a scientifically answerable question at all. Instead, our relationship was a friendship based on a common interest in talking and enjoying good food. I am also delighted to say that she liked my sense of humor, and I could almost always get her to laugh. She liked the imitations I used to do of her and sometimes would even get me to perform them for others.

In 1983, Elisabeth purchased my farm in Headwaters, Virginia. It reminded her of her childhood home in Switzerland, and she was happy as a lark out there.

After Elisabeth died, a journalist telephoned and asked me for a comment on her death. My son Samuel, who was visiting me, overheard my end of the conversation, so he chimed in with his reminiscences. He remembered Elisabeth reading stories to him many times when he was a little boy and she came to visit us.

That is how I remember her also, as a kindhearted friend, who, of course, was somewhat difficult and irascible at times, too. But that was just part of her charm and lovability, as all of us who knew her can testify.

Since she passed away, from time to time I have experienced a bit of regret that she and I never did get around to talking about death and dying and life after death. If I could go back and redo anything in my relationship with Elisabeth, I believe that would be it.

Dr. Raymond Moody is a world-renowned scholar and researcher, and is the leading authority on the near-death experience, a phrase he coined in the 1970s. He is the bestselling author of 12 books, including *Life After Life,* which has sold over 10 million copies. He is Director of The Raymond Moody Research Foundation, a non-profit organization dedicated to learning, teaching, exploring, and developing techniques for understanding what happens when we die.

In You I Have Lit a Candle

By Cathleen Fanslow-Brunjes, R.N., M.A., C.N.S.

A fellow pioneer who has toiled in the field of death and dying for 44
years shares how Elisabeth changed her life.

The summer of 1972 is indelibly etched in my heart and memory:
I met Elisabeth Kübler-Ross, and my life was changed forever.
I was one of 11 students who attended her two-week Death and Dying workshop at the University of Chicago. Elisabeth had the gift of
making you feel as if you were the only person in the room, and I felt
her words were meant just for me.

At the end of the workshop, Elisabeth invited us to a farewell lunch
at her home. She served six-foot-long sandwiches; we met her two
small children and the family cat; and saw her garden, where plants,
flowers, and vegetables all grew together in happy profusion. Since I
was Brooklyn-born, Elisabeth wanted me to meet her husband, Manny,
who was originally from Greenpoint, Brooklyn, and was the bar-
tender for the day.

"Did Elisabeth tell you how we met?" he queried.

Noting my negative head movement he said, "We shared a cadaver in medical school. I had the upper half (he was a neuropathologist); Elisabeth had the bottom half (dealing with the emotions), and that was that!"

Her parting words to us that day were, "In you I have lit a candle." As I pondered what those words might mean to me, I received one of the most important gifts of my life: Elisabeth Kübler-Ross asked me to stay on and work with her.

For the next two weeks, I was privileged to accompany this remarkable woman as she saw patients and families in the hospital, emergency rooms, and her office. Her actions further illuminated me. She lived what she believed; every word she taught us earlier came alive through her dedication and spirit.

I had been working with the dying in hospitals and at home as a Nursing Sister of the Sick Poor for the prior 15 years, yet my "Elisabeth encounter" became a life-changing experience.

I began to realize that the experience with Elisabeth reset my life's direction, and became the guiding light of my work. From that moment on, the quality and understanding of my listening presence with the dying and their families became clear. I understood what it meant to truly accompany the dying on their final journey and the courage it took to do it as Elisabeth had shown me.

My next experience with Elisabeth was in 1974, as part of a committee to organize the Connecticut Hospice, the first American hospice. Whenever I felt my candle growing dimmer from the intensity of my work with the dying, I would phone or write her about my challenging hospice patients and their families. No matter how long it took, she always responded, and I was enlightened.

In 1977 Elisabeth established Shanti Nilaya in California, as head-quarters for the original "Shanti Project," which was to educate people about the hospice concept and end-of-life care. I communicated with her about starting this on the East Coast as a way of spreading the light she had ignited in me.

In the early 1980s I, along with several hospice friends and professionals, established one of the first Shanti Projects on Long Island in New York. This work laid the foundation for the many hospice programs in that area. I spoke with Elisabeth often during this time and she supported me, always encouraging me to keep my candle burning brightly.

After the West Coast Shanti Project closed, she opened the Elisabeth Kübler-Ross Center in Headwaters, Virginia. In 1991, the Nurse Healers Professional Associates International, the official umbrella organization of Therapeutic Touch, chose Elisabeth to receive the Healer of the Year award. As her student and colleague, and a Therapeutic Touch teacher and practitioner, I had the honor of giving her the award. The memory I treasure was the opportunity to honor Elisabeth in this way and to spend the evening with her and the co-founders of Therapeutic Touch, Dolores Krieger and Dora Kunz.

I was invited to share time with her again in 1994 when she spoke at the Learning Annex in New York City. At this time, I was exposed to the irascible side of Elisabeth, and I had the sense that I had finally arrived. She could say anything to me and I would still be there.

Her humanity wasn't always easy to take, but she was a role model encouraging me to be true to my inner light, and never be a "phony baloney" to myself or anyone else. I had planned to volunteer at her headquarters in Virginia, but unfortunately the facility was burned to the ground, which deeply affected Elisabeth for a long time.

I continued to write and call her, as my friends were her hospice nurses in Scottsdale, Arizona. In 1997, the Nurse Healers again honored Elisabeth, and she allowed a small group of us to bring the greetings of the Nurse Healers to her at her home. My heart jumped for joy as I had missed seeing her at the ceremony. When she gave me her "E.T." greeting and our fingers touched, I felt her light instantly fill me to overflowing.

I realized how deeply we had connected those many years ago. I came to understand — on a soul level — what she had done for me and for the thousands whose lives and deaths I have touched in the 33 years since she came into my life. This was all because she said, "In you I have lit a candle."

Thank you, Elisabeth. My light continues to shine for the dying, the bereaved, and those who love and care for them.

Cathleen Fanslow-Brunjes is an internationally known expert in the areas of death and dying, and is recognized as a pioneer in the hospice movement. She worked at the first certified hospice program in Long Island, New York, and was instrumental in establishing the first free-standing hospice in Switzerland.

Spreading Hope, Love, and Dignity

By J. Donald Schumacher, Psy.D.

Just one encounter, that's all it took, and another soul who was open
to change embraced his true life path.

In April of 1975, I was invited to attend a lecture on death and
dying being delivered by Swiss psychiatrist Elisabeth Kübler-Ross.
Death and grief had always been of interest to me due to some unre-
solved early losses. I was, however, anxious about facing them. Reluc-
tantly, I agreed to go.

I could never have imagined how that lecture, delivered by a tiny,
self-effacing, and delightful woman, would change my life. Indeed,
that afternoon, my feet were placed on a path that led me to a lifelong
passion and commitment to promoting better care for the dying.

Elisabeth was confident that there was a better way to die. After
that first lecture, I attended many of her famous workshops where
healthcare professionals and dying patients would meet and process
the impact of our past and current losses on our lives.

One special afternoon involved a ride through the Rocky Mountains in a van carrying 10 people, five of whom were actively dying. Elisabeth instructed me to pull up to a beautiful stream; all of us, some having to be carried, entered the water. We played and cried and laughed for an hour, all relishing our humanity and confronting our fears.

It was the most precious moment. When we returned to the hotel, we all went to Elisabeth's room for tea. We continued the thoughtful and supportive conversations begun in the stream. The afternoon became the seminal event in my personal healing. Unbeknownst to me at the time, my professional life was being formed.

The heartfelt moments, the conversations, the laughter, and the tears have all shaped my life. As the president and chief executive officer of the National Hospice and Palliative Care Organization, I have the opportunity to continue to spread Elisabeth's message of hope, love, and dignity. I will be forever grateful to her for the friendship and influence she has had in my life.

Dr. J. Donald Schumacher is the president and chief executive officer of the National Hospice and Palliative Care Organization, president of the National Hospice Foundation, and also president of the Foundation for Hospices in Sub-Saharan Africa. He has lectured nationally on the psychological care of terminally ill patients and the need for expansion of hospice care nationally and internationally.

Facing Death with a Smile

By Stefan Haupt

The Swiss filmmaker who directed a documentary of
Elisabeth's life shares some memories from the week
spent with her during production.

After reading Elisabeth's book *The Wheel of Life,* I felt a strong
urge to get in touch with her, and to ask whether it might be
possible to do a documentary film project on her and her life. Death,
as a topic, had interested me since my youth.

I remember how strange it was for me at the age of 18 to realize
that I had never come in contact with a dead body, and how years
later I was so deeply affected when I saw my grandmother standing in
front of the open coffin that held my grandfather's body. She was
holding his hand, and with great tenderness she thanked him again
and again for their life together, and then she said goodbye to him.

It took quite some time to get Elisabeth's phone number, and the
journalist who finally gave it to me said, "You have to be lucky and hit
the right day. She can be quite difficult at times."

Well, after only a few words on the phone from my side, Elisabeth said, "I never say no to a Swiss person; so when do you come? You must hurry, since I don't know whether I'll make it until Christmas. And bring some Läckerli along, Swiss cookies, the ones from the Migros, a special Swiss store. I like those the best."

I visited her in 1999, together with a cameraman, at her home in Scottsdale, Arizona. We spent five days in very open, interesting, lively, and often humorous talks.

I realized that the subject of death provokes fear: fear of one's own death, or the death of one's parents, one's partner, or even one's own children. Alongside this fear, however, can exist a sense of how meaningful and valuable it can be to occupy oneself with the topic of death and dying right in the middle of one's life, not waiting until death seems near or until a serious illness forces the question. I was convinced that death is not just a topic for the elderly or the terminally ill.

The way Elisabeth dealt with this question impressed me. There was no big fuss about the subject, and there was no denying of its sharpness, either. It was just the most natural and obvious thing, that death is a part of life, and that it needs to be discussed, accepted, and honored. The way she was able to talk about it, also about her own death, was so open and natural.

I asked her what she imagined the reactions of her loved ones would be when she died. Her answer revealed much of her humor and the direct manner in which she talked about all the details without reservation.

She answered, "My daughter has a terrible hang-up about cremation, so I promised her she could bury me. I bought a plot of land. I bought a coffin. Everything's already paid for. Then I told her to have a big party. There will be food, and everyone can talk and then go outside and release E.T. balloons.

"When one woman heard me mention E.T. balloons, she said, 'That's prohibited. It's copyrighted.'

"I said nonsense. I'll call Steven Spielberg. So I called him. A few minutes later, I had permission to have E.T. balloons made without any legal issues. I did have them printed right away so they wouldn't be able to say later on that for some reason I couldn't do it.

"I know a fine black pastor. He's been a good friend for years. He was my colleague in Chicago. I taught him all about my work. He's one of the few priests I trust. He follows his heart, not his mind. So I asked him to speak at my funeral, and he said yes."

At another time I asked about Elisabeth's current state of health and mind. She enjoyed telling of her attempts to learn, in small steps, what she believed she still needed to master in this lifetime: self-love, surrender, and acceptance. She found it "bloody difficult," and hated it, but said she would rather learn it now, so that when she made the transition, she would never have to come back again.

She said that at death she would go dancing through all the galaxies, and then added with great feeling and delight that she was already looking forward to that.

And then she laughed, surprisingly and mischievously. I enjoyed that moment so much that I put it at the end of my documentary of her life, *Facing Death*. This way all the people who viewed the film would leave the theater with a smile.

The week I spent with her during production of the film is a precious memory that I will always keep, combined with deep gratitude for her life and work. Thank you, Elisabeth, from the bottom of my heart. Have a good flight and fantastic dances through all the galaxies of this immense universe.

Stefan Haupt of Fontana Film GmbH in Zurich, Switzerland, is an award-winning director of feature films and documentaries. His documentary on Elisabeth Kübler-Ross, *Facing Death,* was nominated for the Best Swiss Film Documentary in 2003; received the Study Award from the Swiss Federal Office for Culture; and was a finalist in the 2004 International Health and Medical Media Award, U.S.A.

Changing the Course of My Life

By Caroline Myss, Ph.D.

When internationally known bestselling author and medical intuitive
Caroline Myss was a college student, she was hired to write an
exposé on the "infamous" Elisabeth Kübler-Ross. Her brief
encounter with Elisabeth was to change her life in ways beyond
anything she could have imagined.

I first met Elisabeth Kübler-Ross at one of her workshops in
Appleton, Wisconsin, in 1978. I was a graduate journalism student, and she still resided in Chicago. I attended the workshop, I must
admit, under false pretenses. I was supposed to do an exposé on her
for a Chicago magazine because Elisabeth had begun to create serious
waves at the University of Chicago with all of her death and dying
work.

One incident stood out at the time, and that was her revelation that
while she was working on her resignation from the University of
Chicago, she was visited by a former patient of hers by the name of
Mrs. Schwartz. As Elisabeth was already doing her work with dying

patients, a "former" patient for her meant someone who had, in fact, died.

This story made headlines in the *Chicago Tribune* and I was hired to attend her workshop and do one of those newspaper-type stories in which I would expose her as a fraud. I had never been to a workshop or seminar of any kind before and had absolutely no idea what to expect. Seventy people filled the room and as soon as everyone was seated, this tiny woman walked in and sat in front of the group, cigarettes in hand. I could not believe how petite she was, considering her already powerful reputation.

I was absolutely spellbound the moment she started to speak, although I cannot now recall what she said. Eventually she asked the group to introduce themselves, and one by one, people began sharing the many painful stories of their lives. I was stunned by how open these people were about their most private experiences.

When it was my turn to say something, I said, "My name is Caroline, and I am a graduate student in … theology." Then I sat down, eager to fade into the woodwork. As the workshop continued, I kept waiting, hoping, looking for an opportunity to "interview" Elisabeth in the guise of a casual conversation (that's what undercover reporters do … ha). But no such opening came up.

Meanwhile, my nerves were on edge with all the people who were crying and wailing about their childhoods and bad marriages and betrayals. I wanted to run out of there so fast and never look back. Then, on the last day, just as yet another person was about to start her tale, Elisabeth silenced her and turned her attention to another woman named Caroline.

Elisabeth said, "I know you're thinking of leaving here today, but I won't let you go until you tell this group why you came here in the first place." This woman was over six feet tall, awkward, shy, and frightened half out of her mind. Elisabeth, a five-foot giant, made her come up to the front of the room so that she could address the entire group. She was far too intimidated to do that, so Elisabeth said, "Then sit on the floor with me and just look at me when you speak."

Gently, easily, Elisabeth coaxed this fragile woman into revealing one of the most heartbreaking stories I have ever heard. She was abandoned at age 11; she hid in stores and churches during high school in order to find somewhere to be; she put herself through college; she put herself through graduate school; and one month before coming to this workshop, she completed her master's degree. Two weeks later, she was diagnosed with terminal cancer.

I could not keep the tears from running down my face. I thought my heart would break for this woman. If I had known one way — any way — to help her, I would have been at her side in a New York second. But I felt more helpless in that moment than I had ever felt in my life. I suddenly felt in my gut — not my ordinary gut — but my soul's gut that this woman would be dead by the end of the summer. I wanted that information to go away, to be "just a thought," but it wasn't. It had that "feel" to it that I would eventually come to recognize as the substance of a medical intuitive reading.

After that, all I wanted to do was ask Elisabeth questions about life, death, human consciousness, healing, and spirituality. I had a thousand questions, all of them personal, none of them for the magazine. I managed to get five minutes with her, which felt like the most precious of gifts for me that day. I drove back to Chicago that afternoon, knowing that something profound had shifted in me, but I wasn't exactly certain what that something was.

By the time I arrived home, I had a fever of 102 degrees and could barely talk because of a sore throat. I hadn't even noticed that I had become so ill. I was still living at home with my parents because I was in graduate school. As I was debriefing with Mom about the extraordinary workshop I had just attended, I suddenly said, "I am not going to be a journalist. I will never be a journalist. I need to pursue something in that other world. I don't know what, but I know I must study the human spirit."

And that was that, as they say. I switched my major to theology. I never wrote another news story — certainly not one to expose Elisabeth Kübler-Ross. She was my doorway into the world of human consciousness, medical intuition, and energy medicine. I adored her from that time on, and always will. She gave so much so that others might have an easier journey in this life, and she personally suffered a great deal behind the scenes. Hers was not an easy life at all. I hope that when she passed over, she was greeted by all those she helped into the spirit world. She was, without a doubt, one of the most courageous souls of our era.

Dr. Caroline Myss is internationally known as a medical intuitive and has taught in 35 countries around the world. Four of her books have been on the *New York Times* bestselling list: *Anatomy of the Spirit,* which was published in 18 languages, as well as *Why People Don't Heal and How They Can, Sacred Contracts,* and *Invisible Acts of Power.*

> *"I can assure you that the greatest rewards in your whole life will come from opening your heart to those in need."*

— Elisabeth Kübler-Ross, M.D.

Trusting the Process

By Stephen Levine

Bestselling author Stephen Levine affirms his deep affection for
Elisabeth, and acknowledges that the defining experience in his life
and career was his association with her.

When I first met Elisabeth Kübler-Ross in 1976, I was leading
a workshop with fellow author and spiritual teacher Ram
Dass. After an afternoon's meditation, she invited me to attend one
of her five-day workshops. I quickly agreed, and attended several. At
one of these workshops, I received a calling to serve the dying. I knew
that to be a caregiver could be heartbreaking and exhausting. I thought
it would be helpful to offer meditation teachings specifically for them.
I wanted to do it with Elisabeth as part of her workshops. I decided I
would ask about this the next time we were together.

Soon after, when she was visiting California, I experienced one of
those days of repeated near misses. I was anxious that I wouldn't have

an opportunity to talk with her. Finally, we connected. I asked her what she felt about the possibility of my teaching with her.

She said without hesitation, "Well, if it feels right to you and it feels right to me, then it must be right."

I worked with Elisabeth for a few years. She first initiated me into the joy and heartbreak of working with the terminally ill while we were teaching in Houston. She invited me to come with her to visit a young woman named Dierdra, who was dying. It seemed an ideal opportunity to see her work one-to-one with her patient.

But she had other ideas. As we entered the hospital room, I looked about for a chair so I could sit quietly in a corner and observe. Instead, Elisabeth guided me into the only chair beside the dying woman's bed. It was Elisabeth who silently retreated into the corner. There was nothing I could say that felt right. All my methods were obstacles to our connecting. I sat quietly next to the patient for a while. Finally, I just picked up her hand and let our breaths find their natural rhythm together. As I took her breath into my body, we softened into the moment. Dierdra began to speak. She said she was tired of fighting death. She was tired of so many operations, so many last-ditch experiments.

I told her with her remarkable heart that death would not be a problem. She replied, "I know."

Exhausted as she was, it seemed she was blessing me. There was a quality to the shared silence that I had known only in the meditation hall. I do not remember all that was said, but I do remember the heart-joining silence, our breath, and the nearly overwhelming ocean of compassion on which the scene was floating. And the words, less faint all the time, rose in my heart from some distant memory of the Native American tradition: One heart, all same!

I believe that I was drawn toward this work because so much help-lessness could coexist with so much trust in the process. I remember when I was first teaching with Elisabeth how much I appreciated hear-ing her often say, "Nothing is too good to be true!" It gave me a sense of unlimited possibility. It helped me find the light whose blockage we call shadow. It authenticated the miracle of our potential. Indeed, nothing is too good to be true.

In the dedication of the book I was writing at the time, I wrote:

> "I would like to dedicate this book to my dear friend Elisabeth Kübler-Ross who, in one of those cosmic coin-cidences in which she so delighted, died within hours of the completion of this book, *Unattended Sorrow: Recover-ing from Loss and Reviving the Heart,* the last in a series of books on the subject she initiated me into 30 years ago."

We meet a few people along the way who change our lives. May all who read this find what I found in Elisabeth.

Stephen Levine's bestselling books *Healing Into Life and Death, A Gradual Awakening* and *A Year to Live* are considered classics in the field of conscious living and dying. He and his wife and spiritual partner, Ondrea, have counseled the dying and their loved ones for more than 30 years. Together they wrote the acclaimed *Embracing the Beloved* and *Who Dies?*

A Love Letter to Elisabeth

By Hetty Rodenburg, M.D.

Hetty Rodenburg, Elisabeth's workshop facilitator in New Zealand, has lived a full and successful professional life. Yet, one of her singular accomplishments may be that in her ability to recognize Elisabeth's gift to humanity, she was able to love and accept Elisabeth unconditionally. In a life lived amid controversy and in perpetual motion, this was surely a rare and nourishing balm to Elisabeth's soul.

Elisabeth, how do I sing the song of my soul in a letter? How do I capture freedom of spirit in words?

How do I write about your wisdom, which effortlessly found my imprisoned soul and invited me into a round of truth, creating a space where every breath felt like a safe and new beginning?

Meeting you was a moment frozen in time. A soul decision made eons ago, and my life, my being, will never be the same again.

Elisabeth, I want you to know the love and respect I have for you, and the gratitude I feel for you having taught and guided me to an awareness of my own inner wisdom.

Thank you for all the laughs we shared, for the stories you told me, for the cigarettes we smoked together, and for the "good" chocolates we enjoyed. Thank you for the moments of vulnerability you shared with me when you were ill.

There are two stories I want to remember. You know them both. You were there.

In 1994 I had the great fortune to be asked to staff a five-day residential workshop in Harare, Zimbabwe. This would ultimately prove to be your last workshop outside the United States. You requested 50 percent white and 50 percent black participants, and the majority of the black people were HIV positive.

I was intensely moved by their stories of suffering, loss, and pain, and yet there was an acceptance of life, quite foreign to the Western mind and ways of coping.

During one of the sessions, a black woman told her story, a story with so much loss and pain. I was completely overcome and listened with tears in my eyes, wondering if God had been absent for some time in this woman's life.

You sat there, Elisabeth, listening and at the end of her story, you turned to me and said, "You work with her."

I felt complete and utter panic. "I can't do this," I thought. "Only Elisabeth is capable of working with her."

The woman came to me. Before I could turn around to walk with her to the work area, you stood in front of me. You looked into my eyes and said, "You can do this."

At that moment everything changed. My fear just disappeared, and there was only compassion and love for another human being.

While I was sitting with the woman, listening to her story and her sobbing, I felt God's presence in the room. As you believed in me, Elisabeth, I felt God did also.

A few years ago I decided I wanted to visit you. I wanted to let you know how meeting you had changed my life, and how much my work with dying patients and the presentations I gave were influenced by your teachings, your philosophy, and the principles you advocated.

Together with Johanna Treichler, a fellow staff member and friend, I flew to Phoenix and set off into the desert.

When we arrived at the house, an ambulance was just driving away. Your son, Ken, told us that you had fallen out of bed the previous night and had just been found by a woman who delivers Federal Express packages.

When we arrived in the emergency room of the hospital, I had to look behind several curtains before I found you, Elisabeth. You were lying all by yourself on a trolley in a dark, barren room.

You looked so frail and small. I remember the sadness I felt seeing you, this icon of the medical world, the renowned physician known to millions, alone without any nursing assistance or comfort.

The caregiver in me took over. I ran around to find warm blankets and pillows, which Johanna and I tucked in around your frail body.

"I want a drink," you said.

I got a can of cold lemonade, and placed my arm around your head and shoulders to give you the drink.

You screamed at me in Swiss-German, which unfortunately my Dutch education had not included, and I kept pouring the drink into your mouth.

Luckily Johanna, who does understand Swiss-German, returned, and pointed out to me that the drink was running simultaneously into your mouth and down your neck!

Mea culpa, Elisabeth, mea culpa.

We dried you and got a clean, warm sheet.

As you relaxed, I thought about how, back in New Zealand, I had envisaged this meeting with you. I visualized all the wonderful things I would say to you, Elisabeth.

But life presents us with its own script. Now here we were, Johanna and I sitting, like guardians, on both sides of you in a darkened hospital room. I suddenly remembered your teaching: "The gift is in the giving; do not attach your expectations to that gift."

You were still teaching me, Elisabeth!

Suddenly the curtain was pulled away, the light switched on and there he was:

A doctor in a stark white coat, with a benevolent, confident smile radiating beams of bright light.

You opened your eyes. You saw something white in all that light and to our astonishment you sat up, raised your right arm, and pointed at this figure. "Jesus!" you called out.

There was absolute silence.

Surprise swept over the doctor's face, but not displeasure.

Johanna said, "No, Elisabeth, just a doctor."

I'll never forget your look, the disappointment, your hope for a fast and final exit completely dashed.

Slowly the reality, the room, your body, all of us came back into your consciousness.

You sighed, Elisabeth, and closed your eyes. You knew there were many miles to go before you could go home.

Elisabeth, how can mere words do justice to such a gift to mankind? I offer you simply my undying love and respect.

Dr. Hetty Rodenburg received her medical degree from Leyden University in Holland and went to New Zealand to begin her medical practice in 1971. She worked and trained with Elisabeth, and facilitated her workshops there and in Europe until 2001. She is in private practice counseling those diagnosed with life-threatening illnesses, as well as teaching and facilitating seminars.

Remember, Elisabeth?

By Johanna M. Treichler, M.A.

The power of four words that Elisabeth spoke to Johanna
transformed her life and set her on a path of service to humanity.

Sooner or later, either on the telephone or during our visits, I would utter, "Remember, Elisabeth?" Then my conversations with Elisabeth would revert to the past, to memories of our work and travels. We had good times together! Elisabeth was able to travel down memory lane with me until her very last months.

When these stories brought a smile to her face and when her eyes sparkled, I felt happy. It was a way to show my mentor my deep appreciation for her time spent with me. For me personally, it was also a wonderful way to relive unforgettable moments of that special era of my life with Elisabeth.

As thousands of individual lives have been touched and changed by meeting Elisabeth, so my life was altered. I met the so-called death and dying lady in early 1983. However, Elisabeth was so much more than that label. She really was a life-coach, teaching anyone who was willing to change, how to truly live life to its fullest potential. She offered ways to look at and deal with repressed issues — what Elisabeth called "unfinished business."

It was the weight of my "unfinished business" that made me go to one of Elisabeth's five-day workshops called Life, Death, and Transition. Elisabeth developed these workshops to help people heal on any level they needed. Through her experience of listening to dying individuals, she realized how personal sharing and witnessing in a nonjudgmental environment were at the core of grieving and healing, of letting go and moving on with life.

This healing process was so deeply transformative for me that I wanted to do this kind of work and help others. Even though I had no background in psychology or as a health-care professional at that time, Elisabeth encouraged me to go through her training program.

Maybe being a Swiss immigrant myself, having similar interests, and being a hard worker like Elisabeth allowed me this opportunity. I don't know. I just knew that we worked really well together.

Elisabeth's support and acceptance changed my life. I still have a little card she gave me in 1985, on which she wrote, "I believe in you!"

Over a period of 10 years, I worked in English-speaking and German-speaking countries as one of the staff facilitators at workshops and training programs for the Elisabeth Kübler-Ross Center.

She enjoyed introducing me to new cultures and places as far away as the north of Alaska and the south of Australia. It was also a privilege to work with Elisabeth in our native Switzerland. One of our favorite workplaces was the retreat in St. Gerold, Austria, where over the years thousands of European participants came to meet Elisabeth.

In our travels I often held the role of secretary, shopping consultant, hairdresser, and "bodyguard." I saw how fame could be difficult. People recognized Elisabeth everywhere. Individuals would come up to her on the street, in restaurants or shops, even in bathrooms, telling her how her books or lectures had helped them, or asking for advice.

As Elisabeth valued her privacy, at times I had to help her be "Mary Smith," which was her pseudonym of choice.

Elisabeth was a small, powerful woman, with wispy hair and sparkling, attentive eyes behind her spectacles. She loved to wear comfortable clothing and shoes. As small and modest as she appeared, her presence was known whenever she entered a room.

I remember her knitting, with cigarettes and chocolate nearby, always listening, counseling, teaching, or sharing stories about her fascinating and challenging life.

Elisabeth usually worked 18-hour days. She was demanding of herself and of the people working for her. Elisabeth moved methodically and steadily, and always with a plan and purpose.

Elisabeth was incredibly intuitive. She used her gift of seeing things symbolically to tune into others' psyches. On an uncanny level, she always knew what needed to be said or done. I found it fascinating to watch her guide people gently through their pain to new understanding and healing. She was an incredible teacher, a most generous mentor.

After her debilitating strokes, Elisabeth seemed to lose many of her incredible gifts and abilities. But no matter how difficult life was in her confinement — and she expressed her despair, her anger, and her pain in clear terms — still, she always remembered to ask how my life was going, how my family was. When I told Elisabeth about my brother's total paralysis due to A.L.S., she talked about how much better off she was — she could still talk, eat, use her hands, and move around. I was deeply touched.

It was good to visit Elisabeth at her home in Scottsdale, and later, in her assisted-care facility. Even though it was hard to see her trapped in her tired, ill body, her spirit was alive, at times fighting and lamenting, at other times just appreciative and loving. Elisabeth always ended a visit or call with: "Thank you! Love You!"

Thank *you,* Elisabeth! Love *you!*

Johanna Treichler worked with Elisabeth for 10 years, teaching workshops in English-speaking and German-speaking countries. Born in Lucerne, Switzerland, she and her husband Ernie emigrated to Southern California in 1966.

My True Education

By Bernie Siegel, M.D.

The bestselling author of *Love, Medicine and Miracles* recounts his experience with Elisabeth in her workshops, and how they enhanced his life and career.

I started group therapy sessions for cancer patients in 1978. The name of the group was, and is, Exceptional Cancer Patients. This was to help me deal with the problems surrounding death, which wasn't included in my medical education, and to help me care for the group members in a therapeutic way.

In 1979 I was thrilled to attend an Elisabeth Kübler-Ross workshop titled Life, Death, and Transition. I was in awe of Elisabeth, and I can still hear her voice saying, "Burrnee." That workshop was the beginning of my true education and my relationship with Elisabeth. I believe I was the only doctor there as a participant. I recall sitting and listening to everyone introduce themselves and sharing their pain. When my turn came, I was ready to burst. I moved to center stage to tell everyone about my pain and trouble relating to my practice and family. I was angry about my life and how unfair it seemed. When I was done, Elisabeth asked me, "Do you hate?"

I said, "Yes."

Then she turned to the group and asked, "Do you think he hates?"

Everyone answered, "No."

Then she turned to me and spoke a few simple words that have stayed with me all these years: "You have needs, too."

My next lesson, and again something that has become a major part of my life and work, came from a drawing Elisabeth asked me to do. I drew an outdoor scene with crayons and showed it to her. She told me the meaning of colors and images, which gave me a great deal of needed insight into my life. I went back to my practice and made the drawings an important part of patient care.

I was disturbed by what I realized I had not been taught in medical school about Jung's work and how dreams and drawings can reveal somatic aspects and diagnoses of physical as well as emotional illness.

When I learned about other Jungian therapists from Elisabeth, I wrote them about what I had discovered, and they wrote back saying, "calm-down-we-know-this." Medical journals refused my articles, saying they were interesting but inappropriate. The Jungian journals said they were appropriate but not interesting.

Because of Elisabeth, I began to study the works of people like Susan Bach, Gregg Furth, and others. As a result, a whole new world opened up that I have been trying to share with the medical profession ever since.

Elisabeth also talked about near-death experiences, life after death, and much more. I went back to the hospital and started talking to patients who were under anesthesia and observed the positive effects of the communication.

Oh, I was considered crazy in those days, especially after one emergency case when my patient's heart stopped. The anesthesiologist felt it was hopeless and started to leave the room. Because of Elisabeth, I said out loud to the patient, "Tom, it's not your time yet! Come on back!" His heart started to beat again, and he recovered from the surgery.

Elisabeth opened my life and mind, and taught me to accept what I experienced.

I attended other retreats when Elisabeth was in the Northeast and even had her come and speak to a packed auditorium at Yale Medical School in the early 1980s.

I remember her coming to our home and then driving her to the airport. We stopped along the way so she could get out of the car to smoke. That was the one thing that always confused me: her desire to help people live until they died, and yet she continued to smoke.

Elisabeth and I attended the opening of the first inpatient hospice in the U.S., in Branford, Connecticut. Her groundbreaking work in the field of death and dying had helped make it possible. They had set up a special, light-filled room where people could express their feelings in a safe environment. They also had a nursery school because Elisabeth felt that children and those who were dying could help teach each other about life.

One of the things I had to laugh about was how angry Elisabeth was when her physical health started to deteriorate. I remember calling her and she was in a rage. I told her she needed to attend an Elisabeth Kübler-Ross workshop. I don't know if that helped or not, but I do know she made the transition to acceptance.

Another interesting recent event concerning Elisabeth was a phone call from Monica, a friend of mine who is a medium. Monica does not live near me or know about recent events in my life. Her calls are spontaneous and meant to help guide me and the people I know. My mother had died a few months before this call, but Monica did not know that. She called to tell me that my mom and dad were together again and were very happy and proud of me.

She then went on to say, "There is a woman showing them around, making it easier and entertaining them. She likes chocolate and smokes cigarettes. Do you know who it is?"

A few minutes later Monica said, "Oh! It's Elisabeth Kübler-Ross."

Elisabeth, God bless you and thank you. You have been a guide to me and my family in this life and now the next one. I look forward to our next get-together, but I don't want to rush things.

Dr. Bernie Siegel, a pioneer in holistic medicine, is considered a leading expert in the art of healing. He is a popular lecturer, and the author of many bestselling books, including *Love, Medicine and Miracles, Help Me to Heal,* and *Peace, Love and Healing.*

Captivating, Charismatic, and Smoking

By C. Norman Shealy, M.D., Ph.D.

One of the world leaders in holistic medicine has a little challenge
when Elisabeth's smoke gets in his eyes, lungs and life philosophy.

I first heard Elisabeth at one of the Holistic Health Association
conferences in San Diego. It was shortly after she had come out
of the closet about her guides. She was charismatic, and she capti-
vated an audience of 3,000 people.

In 1980, at one of the early American Holistic Medical Association
meetings, Elisabeth was a keynote presenter. She was speaking in Madison, Wisconsin, first, so we had to fly her in a chartered plane to get her
to the meeting in La Crosse on time. I flew down with the pilot to pick
her up and almost choked on the way back, as she smoked all the way! It
was all we could do to have her not smoke while lecturing. But she was,
of course, charming and delivered a marvelous lecture before she
took off again.

It was my privilege to be with her a number of times after that, as well as to have an ongoing correspondence. Elisabeth was truly one of the most inspiring leaders of the 20th century.

Dr. C. Norman Shealy is the founding president of the American Holistic Medical Association and current president of Holos University Graduate Seminary in Springfield, Missouri, which he also founded.

The Gift of a Returned Life

By John G. Rogers, M.D.

How infinitely fascinating and synchronistic are the circumstances that
conspire to bring an individual meant to meet and work with
Elisabeth — to be drawn into her presence.

Elisabeth gave a talk at Melbourne, Australia's Queen Victoria
hospital in 1983. I went up after the lecture to ask her a question, and she invited me to stay and have coffee and a talk with her.
After chatting for about an hour, I had to go. As I was leaving, Elisabeth
poked me in the chest with a forefinger and said, "You will come to
my workshop."

About one year later, I was sitting at my desk planning a professional trip to the States. I had a spare week and wondered what I
would do with it. My secretary brought in my mail and there was my
first Elisabeth Kübler-Ross newsletter.

I flicked through it and found that a Life, Death, and Transition
workshop was being run in Kamloops, British Columbia, coinciding
with my spare week.

In my role as medical geneticist I did a lot of grief counseling and I felt it would be a good academic exercise to attend. So I signed up and eventually headed off to Kamloops. The only thing I found disconcerting prior to the workshop was a request to bring phone books, which I brought along with my usual array of pads and pens for notes.

While standing in the line to register for the workshop, this small woman, wearing a woven Greek bag over her shoulder, came up, grabbed my wrist, and said, "John it's great to see you here." I turned around to the person behind me in the line and asked, "Who was that?" She said that it was Elisabeth.

The workshop started that afternoon with introductions and drawings, and so far I had not had the opportunity to write any notes, an unusual experience for an academic like me. There was also an emotional tension in the room, the likes of which I had never experienced at other meetings.

The next morning there was a mattress and a stack of phone books in the front of the conference room, which I soon realized were to be hit with a short rubber hose to help release grief and anger. Elisabeth was running the workshop. I found myself on that mattress early in the morning, deeply in touch with grief over the death of my daughter, Emma, and angry about all that had happened in the hospital.

Somehow Elisabeth knew without any words how guilty I felt over the decision I had made to withdraw treatment when I saw that there was no hope for Emma. Elisabeth encouraged me to talk to the group about this and to look for their reaction. After this experience I felt different, much clearer, and less burdened.

At the workshop I met people who became important in my life, in particular Larry Lincoln and Johanna Treichler, who were there as staff members. Elisabeth talked to me before the end of the workshop about taking the training and becoming a staff member.

I felt that I had really connected with an extraordinary lady, who, although famous for death and dying, had given me my life back. We continued to correspond, and she invited me to be a trainee at the workshops that were coming up in Sydney in 1985. I continued my training and facilitating at workshops in Australia and New Zealand.

On New Year's Day in 1989, I was diagnosed as having a lymphoma. I came home from hospital after surgery and chemotherapy and was profoundly shaken and ill. I was disheartened by all that had happened. The phone rang soon after I arrived home and it was Elisabeth, asking how I was and offering some love and prayers. She also wrote an item in her newsletter requesting prayer and support for me. I became aware during my meditation of the love and encouragement that flowed to me from around the world.

I next saw Elisabeth at the First International Conference on Children and Death held in Athens, Greece, later that year. There I discovered the side of Elisabeth that was the intrepid shopper. I would be sitting in the session of the conference and Elisabeth would appear at the door and beckon me.

When I responded to her call, she would say, "Let's go shopping. You will learn a lot more if you come out with me than you'll learn sitting there." And, paradoxically, this was true. We had a great deal of fun going on long walks and exploring the shops. Elisabeth bought me a cowbell to remind me of her and her Swiss origins.

I also visited Elisabeth on the Healing Waters Farm in Virginia. She had already suffered her first stroke, but nonetheless was in good spirits. When I rang to say that I had arrived and was at the guest house, she came down with an apple and apricot pie that she had just baked. I spent some quiet time helping her with Christmas cards and noticed that her home was an extraordinary clutter of photographs and mementos. This was the home that was ultimately burned down, destroying all of Elisabeth's possessions.

I managed to visit Elisabeth a couple of times in her home in Scottsdale and eventually saw her in the nursing home.

I felt very sad at the prospect of seeing Elisabeth in a nursing home. When I first arrived, with her longtime friend Johanna Treichler, she seemed rather flat. But as time passed, her spirit revived, and she became quite feisty and obviously enjoyed our visit.

I continued telephone contact with Elisabeth until it became too difficult for her to manage. There were always love and blessings for me and to all her friends in Australia and a "thank you" for calling.

I felt it was difficult for Elisabeth to grasp how important she had been to so many people over the years. I hope that she reaped the rewards she so richly deserved when she reached the other side. We always finished all visits with: "I'll see you when I'm back in the States, or if not, on the other side," so I expect her to be there waiting for me.

Dr. John Rogers went as a Fellow to Johns Hopkins in Baltimore, Maryland, to study medical genetics. He returned to Melbourne, Australia, in 1976 where he was responsible for the building of the Clinical Genetics Unit, and ultimately became its director. He was a lifelong friend of Elisabeth's and conducted workshops for her in Australia. After being diagnosed with lymphoma in 1989, he retrained as a psychotherapist with a special interest in grief and life-threatening disorders.

The Teacher I Needed

By Susanne Schaup, Ph.D.

Susanne Schaup spent many years translating Elisabeth's books into
German. The universal message became a part of her.
When Susanne was diagnosed with cancer, the opportunity to test
the validity and truth of Elisabeth's work in her own life
emerged before her.

My expectations may have been too high when I met Elisabeth
Kübler-Ross for the first time. She was lecturing in Tucson,
Arizona, where I had stopped to visit friends. I was excited to meet
Dr. Kübler-Ross because for many years I had been translating her books
into German. She had become an important figure in my life. Her work
meant everything to me. I had an ailing mother who suffered from severe depression, and Elisabeth had been good enough to respond to my
request for advice. I didn't know if she ever replied to letters and was
deeply touched that she had taken the time to write me a note.

I had missed her every time she came to Germany for lectures or
workshops and was very excited to meet her in Tucson that evening in

the summer of 1983. I remember the moment she came into the room, a small, plain-looking woman in casual dress.

In a crowd I would not have noticed her. This impression changed immediately when she started to speak. She held everyone spellbound. She spoke for an hour and a half, without once referring to notes, without hesitating or repeating any information. It was a beautiful, inspired lecture. At the end there was thunderous applause, which she acknowledged modestly, almost with impatience. She knew there were people waiting to have a private word with her. A crowd had assembled in front of the podium, waiting their turn.

I, too, stood in line, anticipating the moment when I would be able to introduce myself and tell her how impressed I was with her talk. When the moment came at last, I was in for a shock.

She just did not seem interested. She waved me aside and turned to the next person. It was a humbling experience.

After all, I had come all the way from Germany. I had rendered her message to a German reading public, but she clearly was not interested in meeting me.

It took me a while to get over it, but when the next book came up for translation, I forgot the incident and was as passionately involved in my work as ever. I used to cry over her books and take in deeply the lesson that dying or in blooming health, we should live fully until we die.

Today, I understand her better after serving as a volunteer worker in a hospice facility for a year. As she knew so well, every word we say to a dying person is essential. We learn to listen and to come to grips with our own fear of death. There are lessons to learn; there is love to give and to receive. Every moment is a challenge. I found that I became irritated with ordinary conversations and bored with people who were not in a crisis. Perhaps this is what happened to Elisabeth, too. Years of caring for the dying had simply made her impatient with small talk.

All my intimate encounters with her took place when I translated her books, word for word and meaning for meaning, into German. Yet, the most intimate, the most crucial encounter was still to come.

When I was afflicted with cancer myself, I had to undergo aggressive chemotherapy, which kept me in the hospital for five months and an additional month for radiation. Elisabeth's lessons were the best support I could ever have imagined. I had internalized them to a degree that made it easy to accept my illness and to ask for the message in it for me. Clearly, there was unfinished business. Clearly, some changes had to be made.

During my first cycle of chemotherapy, I realized that I might not survive. There was a tremendous emotional release, which became the first step toward recovery. I had come round to the "other side of fear."

In my illness, soaked in sweat and tears, I finally understood the lesson of love. There is divine love at work in every healing, and to open up to it means to look at the world and myself in a new way. Elisabeth's lesson rang in my heart, as it still does: "Learn to live, learn to live!"

It was my privilege not only to translate her work, but also to test the validity and truth of her message in my own life, through the same illness that had given her so many insights. Without the intimate knowledge of her work, my own cancer would not have been such a profound experience of spiritual growth.

When I came to the United States again, Elisabeth had already died. There was no opportunity in this life to have the kind of talk with her that I had longed for. But as I continue to work with her legacy, our spiritual conversation will not end. She has become a friend and a teacher for life. The best teacher does not have to be the nicest or most agreeable person. In fact, this is quite beside the point.

As Elisabeth used to say, "You may not get what you want, but you always get what you need." Elisabeth Kübler-Ross is the kind of teacher I needed.

Dr. Susanne Schaup is a freelance editor, writer, and translator based in Vienna, Austria. In the late 1970s she began translating Elisabeth's books into German for Kreuz Verlag Publishing. She also edited and translated a number of anthologies of great American classics, including the journals of H.D. Thoreau. Her published works include *Sophia — Aspects of the Divine Feminine,* a short monograph on Elisabeth for her 70th birthday, a book about children in India, and a report of her own spiritual experience with cancer.

Down Under with Elisabeth

By Rita Ward, O.A.M.

As Elisabeth was ready to expand into Australia, Rita Ward appeared.
She would direct all of Elisabeth's activity there, including helping to
establish and manage the first Elisabeth Kübler-Ross
Association in the world.

Many years after I met Elisabeth, I learned that her first contact with Australia was through a Marist priest named Fr. Reg Keating. He was in Chicago studying at Loyola University. They met at a lecture she gave and became friends. One day she asked him to get a certain patient to come to her lecture.

The story goes that he almost kidnapped this person without the hospital's permission and arrived at the lecture hall with the woman still in her hospital bed. At that point, Elisabeth had some idea that Australians were different.

My first introduction to Elisabeth came through her appearance on Australian television in 1976. My husband had died two years before, and I had made it my project to change the attitude of the professional staff members who cared for dying people. I remember crying all the way through the program as I realized this woman knew what I had been talking about.

Later my sister gave me a copy of Elisabeth's book, *Questions & Answers on Death and Dying*. The information in the back of this book indicated she worked at Billings University Hospital in America, and there was a phone number. So I rang the number and asked to speak to her, only to be told she had not worked there for eight years.

They gave me another number. So I rang it and thought I would have to speak to at least three secretaries, but Elisabeth answered the phone. I was dumfounded for a full five seconds and just said simply, "I want to come and work with you!"

She replied, "Okay. Just come!"

I said, "I have no money."

She said, "So what? Just come!"

I applied for a Churchill scholarship but did not get it. Then the director of Lifeline rang one day and asked what I was doing about going to America. He told me if I wanted to go, Lifeline Organization would take up a collection to pay for it. That was September 2, 1977. I had no passport, no visa, but nothing was going to stop me.

I rang Elisabeth, and she told me to be at a workshop that was to take place on September 19th. All she gave me was a phone number, no address. She told me I would find it. I did.

Elisabeth was anxious to know all about Australia as she was making her first trip there in 1978. She came again in 1979 and 1980 and led workshops in various cities.

In 1980-1981 I visited Elisabeth at Shanti Nilaya in Escondido, California, and it was there she asked if I would set up her Australian organization. What she actually asked me to do was to organize six lectures in six cities in Australia.

The fact that I did not know six people in these six places was of no concern to her. I said that I would.

One of the special aspects of my working with Elisabeth was that she would bring her son, Ken, with her, and I adopted him as my American son, while she in turn adopted my son, George, as her Australian son. We had some great, fun times together.

I took Elisabeth to meet my brother-in-law in Townsville because he was a real bushman, and Elisabeth thought that was great. He returned the compliment by saying, "She's not a bad old stick!" That, coming from a bushman, meant that she was accepted and could "boil a billy" with the best of them.

It was also in Townsville that we were arrested. I had obviously broken the traffic law while driving her to the lecture hall. It was raining, and I could not understand why this car was following me until they held up a sign saying "Police."

We had a hard time convincing them that I had to get Elisabeth into the hall to give her lecture, and that I would come back and attend to my misdemeanor. Elisabeth gleefully announced to the crowd that she had traveled all over the world but had to come to Townsville to be arrested.

Looking back, I remember on her first visit to Australia we hadn't completed the official registration of the Elisabeth Kübler-Ross Association. After the lecture I had more than $30,000 in my handbag, which Elisabeth would need to continue her work, but had no legal way to get it out of Australia.

Just by chance, my brother-in-law, who was a bank manager, phoned me and suggested that I get the money to him and he would get it to her, which he did. That's all I know. I was willing to do a lot of things for Elisabeth, but going to jail was not one of them.

I spent over five years organizing Elisabeth's trips Down Under, from 1980 to 1985, and during that time the first Elisabeth Kübler-Ross Association (E.K.R.A.) in the world was established. I enjoyed a close connection with Elisabeth and her family that has endured for more than 28 years.

Elisabeth gave me the inspiration and the courage to get things done in the communities where I have lived, to blaze a trail where none existed, and to change attitudes when it came to caring for dying people and their families.

Today in Australia there are numerous palliative care units, hospices, and academic courses available, all because of the one little lady who dared to listen and to care, and who was willing to wander the world planting seeds and inspiring others to get up and do something.

By her last trip to Australia, I had left the E.K.R.A. to care for my dying father, but I went to see her. There was a huge crowd milling around, trying to get to her. She turned and whispered to me, "Find a back door and get me out of here!"

I am so glad she has found her own back door, and I am sure she is at peace.

Rita Ward was the facilitator and director of activity for Elisabeth in Australia, and a dear friend for almost 30 years. She has received many awards and honors for her numerous achievements, including Australia's Centenary Medal for Distinguished Service and the Order of Australia Medal.

Comfort the Disturbed
and Disturb the Comfortable

By Gregg M. Furth, Ph.D.

Gregg M. Furth was a Jungian psychologist, author, lecturer, and
longtime friend and associate of Elisabeth's who learned a valuable
life lesson from her.

Elisabeth moved like the wind when trying to accomplish tasks,
and expected others to move along at her speed. While experiencing this air stream over the last 35 years, the most important lesson I learned from her was that she always told me to "Just do it."

When I would talk to her about difficulties, challenges, options, and decisions that I had to make, she would say, "That's a good decision. Just do it." Even today when contemplating decisions, I hear her voice urging me to "just do it," to stick my neck out and have little concern for consequences. To me her mantra was, "Comfort the disturbed, and disturb the comfortable. Get out there and push their buttons."

If I were to pass along her wisdom, it would be, "Just do it." Each individual needs to do whatever he or she has been contemplating, imagining, desiring, or wanting to accomplish.

Elisabeth believed in the centering of the Self, to trust one's inner Self and to get on with it — that one should stop hesitating because of negativity, excuses, and fear of failure, rejection, or criticism. Elisabeth could have stopped herself with all the obstacles that she experienced in her work on death and dying, but she stood steady and *just did it*. She did not heed the warnings and the scare tactics that her colleagues and others hammered into her; she just did it. She not only preached these words, she lived them.

I've taken on Elisabeth's mantra and did exactly what she suggested many times in my life. As a result, I had to carry the consequences; occasionally I encountered grave misunderstandings from colleagues, friends, and family, and yet I also experienced positive results from living from my inner core and felt fulfilled. I believed I was finally accompanying my life path. She advised, supported, recommended, and even insisted on me pushing forward for what I thought was ethical and moral, regardless of what others thought or expected of me.

She would just as blithely tell me to write a few pages for her book *Living with Death and Dying*, and that I should "Just do it" while she cooked dinner, and explained to me that it would be great to sell my apartment in New York and move to London.

She believed in the realism of the life within an individual, and that death could not alter this energy and driving force. I am pleased that I had the brains and the courage to take on the opportunity to follow her challenge. And in the end, I realize her courage is what I admired, with all the wisdom that she so easily shared.

She was not perfect. She knew this and admitted it many times to me, but she moved forward carrying courage and conviction that when called from within, "Movement in any direction is better than no movement at all."

And with this, she left this world a better place for us all, because, as she said to many of us before she died, "I did a good job."

Dr. Gregg M. Furth died in 2005 just after the completion of this essay for *Tea with Elisabeth*. He spent the last 35 years of his life counseling emotionally disturbed and terminally ill children and adults. His book *The Secret World of Drawings: A Jungian Approach to Healing Through Art* has been published in six languages. He conducted numerous workshops worldwide on death and dying and therapeutic art methods.

The Ordinary and Extraordinary Meet!

By D. Brookes Cowan, Ph.D., M.S.W.

Breaking centuries-old taboos and deep-seated traditional thinking
was one of Elisabeth's great strengths. She also took childlike
delight in shocking "do-gooders" by defying the
rules of public conduct.

W hen Elisabeth Kübler-Ross came into the world, the axis of
the planet must have shifted a bit. This peanut of a triplet,
full of sassiness and self-confidence, a rebel with a cause, embarked
upon a journey that would ultimately change the world forever. Rely-
ing on her keen intellect, using her strong and true heart as her rud-
der, and her compassion and integrity as her compass, Elisabeth worked
tirelessly on behalf of disenfranchised populations, most particularly
the dying.

Often called the "mother of hospice" in the U.S., Elisabeth brought
dying and death out of the closet and placed them squarely on the public agenda. Her death with dignity movement espoused autonomy and
respect for dying individuals and their families, effective pain control,

attention to emotional and spiritual needs, and the importance of taking care of unfinished business before death.

The first time I met Elisabeth was at a lecture at the University of Virginia in the late 1970s. I was aware even then of the intersection between the ordinary and the extraordinary in her life. Here was this diminutive woman, wearing Birkenstock sandals, a house dress, and thick horn-rimmed glasses, yet as soon as Elisabeth began to speak in that distinct Swiss accent, the ordinariness of the encounter was transformed into an extraordinary event.

She spoke of the time when she announced to her mentor in medical school that she had decided to dedicate her life to work with the dying. His response was to spit on her, turn away in disgust, and inform her that she was wasting a brilliant medical career. As usual, Elisabeth's resolve was not diminished.

After hearing her lecture, I embarked on a career in the field of end-of-life care, becoming one of a million points of light ignited by Elisabeth's flame.

I did not have the opportunity to meet Elisabeth again until 2002, when a number of folks from Vermont and I visited her because of a documentary we were making about the history of hospice. This encounter spawned a very special friendship between the "gang" in Vermont, Elisabeth, and Ken, her son. Little did we know what was in store for us, as we got to know the ordinary human being behind the legend of Elisabeth Kübler-Ross.

Elisabeth often remarked that she had two regrets in life: not being mischievous enough and not having danced enough. Elisabeth was a prankster of the first order, and we soon realized that when her eyes danced, there was something going on. For example, during our second visit to see Elisabeth, the Vermont gang, including camera crew, volunteered to take Elisabeth to her favorite animal park in Scottsdale. We didn't real-

ize that this "icon" who had worked to free Nelson Mandela and counseled royalty in times of grief, was such an iconoclast.

Within hours of our arrival at the park, Elisabeth had playfully picked
up and stashed up her sleeve a handful of polished stones (which we
dutifully put back), defied a no-smoking order at an outdoor restaurant
by being photographed holding three lit cigarettes in her hand, and finally, was busted by the park police for feeding giraffes her Ritz crackers,
despite the large posted sign that read: "Do not feed the animals!"

Elisabeth reveled in her social defiance and mercilessly labeled us
cowards and do-gooders for being worried about the consequences of
her actions. However, we soon learned we could win back her affection with Swiss chocolate (not candy) and lobster!

One of the other extraordinary qualities Elisabeth possessed was
her uncanny ability to sniff out those who were authentic and those
who were "phony baloneys." Her friends knew that Elisabeth divided
the world into those two camps, and those of us who passed the test
could be certain of where we stood with Elisabeth. It was often in the
corner, for having said something stupid or Republican.

For those of us who loved Elisabeth, it was difficult witnessing her
struggle to learn her final two life lessons — patience and unconditional self-love — lessons she said she needed to learn in order to
move on.

During a visit with Elisabeth in June 2004, I asked her how she was
doing with her lessons. She announced that she had finally learned patience because her circumstances left her no choice. She was still, however, struggling with unconditional self-love.

At 8:10 p.m. on Tuesday, August 24, 2004, her final lesson was learned
as I, along with David Kessler, her children, Barbara and Ken, witnessed
Elisabeth's transition. The butterfly, its wings having been strengthened
by the struggle to exit the cocoon, gracefully emerged from its chrysalis

and took flight, headed for "a world more loving and glorious than we can imagine."

Despite her protestations, Elisabeth was a star of the first magnitude, whose light raised the consciousness of humanity and brought the topics of dying and death out of the darkness.

Though Elisabeth's star has been transformed, its light cannot and will not disappear. It is the responsibility of each of us to carry Elisabeth's light into the shadows of fear and ignorance so that everyone, in every corner of the world, will have the opportunity to die on his or her own terms, peacefully, without pain, surrounded by family and friends. The extraordinary Elisabeth Kübler-Ross did ultimately achieve a death with dignity, the kind of passage that the most ordinary of human beings deserves.

Thank you, Elisabeth, for all you have given to us and to the world. May you "dance across the galaxies" forever.

Dr. D. Brookes Cowan, a medical sociologist and gerontologist, has taught in the Sociology Department at the University of Vermont since 1983. As chair of the Madison-Deane Initiative, she was involved in the making of the critically acclaimed documentary *Pioneers of Hospice: Changing the Face of Dying,* which featured Elisabeth Kübler-Ross among others. Dr. Cowan had the privilege of being called to Arizona to coordinate Elisabeth's care during the last week of her life.

*"The only thing that lives
forever is love."*

—— Elisabeth Kübler-Ross, M.D.

My Journey with Mom

By Ken Ross

Elisabeth's son shares some uncommon memories of childhood
and his insightful appreciation for the work his
mother was called to do.

The first thing that occurred to me when I thought about writing this commentary was how to explain the many life-changing experiences with my mother. How does anyone explain his or her parents, what they mean to our lives, and what they shared? Then I wondered how I could possibly condense 44 extraordinary years with my mother into a designated number of words.

I was only nine years old when my mother wrote her first book, *On Death and Dying*. After that, my sister and I had to share Mom with the world. I'm good at sharing (I think) so I didn't mind. The frequency of her trips soon increased, as did their length.

It evolved that the best way to spend quality time with her would be to travel with her. So I would look at her extensive travel schedule and choose two places to join her each year.

This was quite an adventure at that young age. It became quite normal to jet off with her to Japan, Australia, Egypt, Brazil, Zimbabwe, Eskimo villages in Alaska, and other exotic destinations.

During those trips, I saw the importance of what my mother did. I realized the incredible impact she had on people she touched by her work, and I understood why she couldn't be home like our friends' mothers.

I watched with amazement as the auditoriums filled with hundreds and thousands of people needing to hear her message.

My mother would get nervous if she saw me at a lecture so she requested that I remain out of her view. Since virtually no one in attendance knew I was her son, I could hide in the back or walk around the lobby. I could anonymously walk around beforehand, during the break and after her lectures listening to participants' comments about what they heard.

I loved hearing people's stories. The audience would come out of her lectures completely transformed. In the short space of a few hours, many would seem to come to terms with the death of a parent or child, something that they might have been haunted by for many years. Some would swear to dedicate their lives to helping the dying, or living their lives in peace and commitment to others.

One woman in Sydney, Australia, called my hotel room and confessed that she had been planning to commit suicide before the lecture. After hearing my mother's talk and subsequently seeing a butterfly (my mother's favorite symbol of transformation), she decided she wanted to live and become a hospice nurse.

It is still difficult for me to grasp the sheer magnitude of the number of lives my mother affected during her life. The stories I heard from around the world seep into my mind every day.

Although she "belonged" to the public, and the actual physical time she could spend with us wasn't extensive, she remained VERY much our mother. She would come home between trips, cooking and baking enough to last us for two weeks. Naturally, she would also be busy answering mail, packing a suitcase for the next trip, and returning telephone calls, but she always made time for activities with us.

Some of the typical activities we would do included candle making, fruit picking (apples, blueberries, raspberries), gardening, and shopping. She was a mad shopper. My sister and I quickly learned not to touch anything in a store, as she would instantly want to buy it for us. I remember once picking up some pigs' knuckles in a butcher shop, and she insisted on buying them for us.

Another favorite memory of my travels with Mom took place in 1980. In Edfu, Egypt, we were taking a horse and carriage ride, and the driver wanted us to meet his family. I was in the courtyard of his apartment complex, and Mom was out front taking photos on the street when she heard a scream from the courtyard. It was simply some children playing, but I will never forget her face as she came charging into the courtyard with her Swiss army knife ready to protect her little boy.

Life with Mom was never boring. We were visiting families of Eskimos in Kodiak, Alaska, who had experienced suicides in the family. I had caught a cold and was sleeping in my hotel room. I woke up to find an Eskimo healer chanting above my head; I thought I was hallucinating. My mother had simply given the healer my room key and told the woman to go do her thing.

As is usually the case, life is filled with ironies and twists of fate. While my mother couldn't be physically present on a full-time basis to care for me during my early years, I spent the last 10 years of her life taking care of her.

After her Virginia house burned down, I brought her to Arizona for some sort of "retirement." (Hah!) Anyone who knows my mother understands that this was no easy task. She was fiercely independent, and despite having had several debilitating strokes, didn't easily accept people telling her what to do. Even in retirement, every day brought boxes of mail, multiple requests, and visitors from around the world.

During her last few years, I took the opportunity to spend an amazing amount of time with her. I would bring her favorite foods, which she received with passion and glee. Everyone knows she liked Swiss chocolate, candies, and tea (Twining, English Breakfast, no milk, two sugars). Yet few, if anyone, would know she also craved a crazy assortment of other foods: Long John Silver's hushpuppies, white-fish salad, Taco Bell's soft-shell beef tacos with extra guacamole, rice pudding, sardines, and blueberry blintzes.

Sometimes I felt like the beleaguered assistant to a temperamental rock star, as I scurried about trying to finish 18 tasks she might assign me. Somehow she would *always* know the one task I might not have finished. She possessed an amazing sixth-sense that went beyond anything most people can imagine.

There are a thousand and one stories to tell about my journey with my mother, but I think this might give you a sense of what it was like to have such a mother. Sometimes it was like being related to a rollercoaster; the "ups" were higher and the "downs" were pretty low sometimes. There were always wild and unexpected turns, ready or not! She taught me so much, not the least of which is to see the world before I leave it. Life is very different now. It's hard to get used to a "normal" life without her.

Ken Ross is an independent commercial photographer based in Scottsdale, Arizona. He specializes in travel-location, people, and corporate photography. His work has been exhibited in the U.S., Japan, and Mexico. His book *Real Taste of Life* was produced in collaboration with his mother and was also released as a calendar. He is currently establishing the Elisabeth Kübler-Ross Foundation to further the work of his late mother.

My Mother's Gifts

By Barbara Rothweiler, Ph.D., A.B.P.P.

Elisabeth's daughter recalls childhood memories and recognizes the
family legacy already evident in her children's lives.

For as long as I can remember, people have asked me, "What is it like to have Elisabeth Kübler-Ross for a mother?" I have never been sure how to answer this question. For me, she was just my mother.

In many ways, she was like many other mothers. Some of my earliest memories include watching her bake and helping her decorate chocolate cakes and sugar cookies, gardening with her when I was about three years old in my own little garden adjacent to hers, and asking repeatedly to hear my favorite story from her childhood.

This was the story about the time she and her sisters took their pet monkey to school, and on the way he jumped off her shoulder into a bakery window, wreaking havoc and causing an incident that was the talk of the village.

We were fortunate to take many family vacations (often including visits to local cemeteries), the plans for which often began with my mother saying, "Let's do something a little crazy."

However, for her, and thereby for my brother and me, just as baking, gardening, shopping, and bedtime stories were basic parts of life, so was death. She spoke of death as commonly as any other topic, at the dinner table or during any family activity. When I was about eight years old, I had a friend sleeping over. My father's uncle, who lived with us, died that evening. My mother, who saw this as an opportunity to show us all how beautiful and peaceful death was, brought us into the room to see him. This was so much like my mother that it seemed "normal."

What I remember next was my friend's mother coming to our house at about midnight to take her home after she had nightmares and had thrown up. My friend's parents, fortunately, understood this event in the manner it was intended and remain in contact with our family to this day.

As a child, I went to work with my mother, which included her early work with children, and later attended her one-week workshops and lectures. I will always remember how easily, comfortably and compassionately she spoke with strangers about very personal topics, including their thoughts on their life and death. I will never forget how she routinely brought audiences of thousands of people to tears in a language that was not her own.

She frequently commented on how much she learned from people as they approached the end of their lives, or those touched by the death and dying of a loved one. She appreciated at a deep level the wisdom she gained from her interactions with them.

I remember dinnertime conversations between my parents about what each thought happened after death. I remember these discussions as playful and humorous, ending in bets about which one would be right and how they would prove to the other that they were right.

I also recall that my mother always wanted to be a grandmother. When I was in high school, much to my embarrassment, she bought me a crib, saying she "just couldn't wait." When my daughters were born (*many* years later), she immediately hopped on a plane, with the help of my brother, to be with us. This was despite the fact that at the time she was unable to walk farther than the distance between her bed and a chair, both of which were in her living room. Nothing could have stopped her.

When we came to Arizona for visits, she had a special tin of miniature Swiss chocolates for my daughters, telling them, "Eat as much as you can." When my daughter Sylvia was in a dance recital, my mother sent me boxes of Kleenex, with a note that said, "I am crying just thinking of watching her." When my daughter Emma was one year old and enjoyed emptying Kleenex boxes, my mother had extras on hand just for Emma to empty. Every phone call from my mother started with, "How are my babies?"

She often said to me, "Tell them every chance you get that I love them so they will never forget." Sylvia's response to that was, "How could I ever forget?" They will never forget.

In interactions with our family, as well as in discussions about her work with others, she shared her value of the importance of treating death as a part of life, frequently saying that children are not afraid if they are not taught to be afraid.

Of the many gifts she gave to us, her family, she gave us the gift of openness about life and death, a respect for teaching and being taught, and a drive to enjoy life.

As she began her journey, in her own words, "to dance in the galaxies," my daughters, Sylvia, five years old, and Emma, two years old, played at the foot of her bed. They were drawing her pictures, telling her stories, and holding her hand. I see her gifts living on in them.

Dr. Barbara Ross Rothweiler works as a rehabilitation psychologist-neuropsychologist in Wisconsin. Dr. Rothweiler and her husband, Jeffrey, are the parents of Elisabeth's two granddaughters, Sylvia and Emma.

I Remember Grandma

By Sylvia and Emma Rothweiler

Following in the footsteps of their grandmother — who was famous
for speaking her truth — Elisabeth's granddaughters announced
that they, too, had something important to say about their "Bama"
and wanted it to be included in this book.

Bama was the best Grandma! She was a really nice lady. She shared chocolate with us. Her favorite color was purple. Purple is Emma's favorite color too. My favorite story is about Chiquito, her pet monkey. She also had pet bunnies when she was little. Me and Emma have a pet bunny just like her. Her bunny's name was Blackie. My bunny's name is Sleighbell. My sister's bunny's name is Carroty. They are brothers. I have a stuffed animal llama like Bama had a real llama. Our llamas have the same name. On her birthday we made her a cactus cake. She loved E.T. She loved me and Emma a lot. She loved her whole family. I miss her.

My name is Sylvia. I am five years old. I go to kindergarten. My teacher's name is Mrs. Koerten. I really like school and my teacher. My favorite part of school is "reading buddies."

My Bama liked to give me chocolate. She liked to eat chocolate just like me. We made a chocolate cake for her on her birthday. It looked like a cactus. You know why we gave her a cactus cake ... because there are cactuses there.

***

My name is Emma. I am three years old. Bama is my Grandma.

***

Editor's note: Somewhere in the galaxies Elisabeth is smiling. All of her life she, too, revered nature, animals, learning, and chocolate ... Swiss chocolate, of course.

Remembering Elisabeth

By Eva Kübler-Bacher

Elisabeth's fellow triplet and only surviving sibling shares
memories of her rebellious sister.

Who else would be better able to write something about
Elisabeth's childhood than me, as I am the only one left from
the Kübler "dynasty."

As everyone knows, we were triplets and Elisabeth was by far the
wildest of the three of us. I remember when she threw a hymnbook into
the face of our awful vicar. The vicar had hit our sister, and Elisabeth was
simply defending Erika. The poor girl and our very strict father had to
show up at the School Committee to apologize for her cheekiness. I also
remember when some foolish boys bothered our sister Erika on the way
back from school. Elisabeth showed no fear and fought them ferociously.

One day Elisabeth and I paired up to do some mischief. The two of us
took our toy bows and arrows and ran around just outside our village.
We annoyed the motorists by shooting at them.

Another vivid memory concerns our monkey "Chiquito." A rich uncle brought him to us from his African trip, and this funny animal was immediately Elisabeth's favorite friend. Of course, she wanted to brag in front of her comrades, and so she put Chiquito on a long leash and we paraded him into the village.

We entered a big bakery owned by a sweet English lady, and the disaster began. Chiquito went totally crazy. With loud yells and shouts he jumped on all the wonderful pastries and cakes in the window, demolishing half of the shop within minutes. It was very difficult for Elisabeth to calm the animal down, but even more challenging was to calm down our father later that evening. The event was the talk of the entire village.

As a punishment, we had to give the monkey to the Zürich Zoo. And there poor Chiquito soon died of homesickness.

What I also remember vividly is my sister as a young pathologist. It was difficult for me to understand why she enjoyed taking apart little frogs, beetles, and other small creatures.

It was equally challenging for her to understand my love of the piano, or our father's stern insistence that his daughters learn to play the piano or some other instrument of their choice. She hated this idea with a passion. Father was a fantastic tenor, and finally I was the one who could accompany him on the piano. My two sisters gave up their piano lessons very quickly, as music was definitely not their thing.

Elisabeth had a great love for nature and the outdoors just as I did. Every year our father took us on a two-week tour over some of the great Swiss Alpine passes. At that time, they were not yet converted into large Alpine streets, but were just little mountaineering paths. Such wonderful events as those a child will never forget.

I believe that this love of nature, instilled in Elisabeth at such an early age, became a foundation of strength that embraced all life, and allowed her to achieve what she did.

Our father was, as I said, a terribly severe father. He would not tolerate any disobedience. My sister Erika and I were obedient, being scared of his punishment, but little rebel Elisabeth, of course, opposed his dictatorial pronouncements at every opportunity. As a result, she was thrown out of the house at the age of 18. On the surface she seemed not to care at all, and simply took a shabby little room in town and followed her dream to become a medical doctor.

It was an interesting twist of fate that when Elisabeth was in her last exams at Zürich University, she received an urgent call from our father asking for her help, as he was deathly ill. Of course, she responded immediately.

As far as physical appearance, we looked very different, yet our ideas and philosophy of life were the same. We enjoyed this intimate connection on many levels until Elisabeth's final day of life.

Eva Kübler-Bacher is a sister of Dr. Elisabeth Kübler-Ross and the only surviving triplet. She emigrated to New York in 1958 and worked for a time at the New York Swiss Tourist Office before returning to Zürich, Switzerland. She and her husband, Peter Bacher, have two daughters, Vreni Aeberli and Susan Elisabeth Bacher.

Tea and Wisdom from Aunt Elisabeth

By Susan Elisabeth Bacher

Elisabeth's niece embraces life lessons through the teachings and examples set by her favorite aunt.

If you wanted to have a cup of tea with *Bettli* (my Aunt Elisabeth), you had to know how she wanted it to be served. Bettli had her own distinctive personal preference: she wanted one bag of Earl Grey, (not to remain too long in the boiling water), one spoon of sugar, and then a little drop of milk. Naturally, of course, this was to be served along with a Dunhill cigarette. Thus prepared, the topics of our conversations just happened intuitively.

For me, Bettli was not only my very favorite aunt, she reminded me of a wise, master teacher. When I sat next to her, the answers that came forth were so clear and honest that I often thought of her as a Native American shaman. Of course, she was too modest to see herself as such, but I know many people saw her that way.

Sometimes she would ask me, "Where is my Swiss chocolate?" If you have ever seen her overloaded and cluttered bedside table, you would know what a difficult undertaking this could be. Fortunately, most of the time she managed to find her chocolate under the piles of books, papers and postcards — and if not — there was always a comfortable stock of Swiss chocolate in the cupboard that would last her for years.

I remember her holding the chocolate with two fingers and with the others the cigarette, which she also enjoyed so much. The ashes on her cigarette would be so long that I would say, "Attention!" She would just look at me and say, "Don't worry."

She held everything in her awareness. No matter what life demanded of her, up until near the end of her life, she was mentally 100 percent present.

I remember she was strong, and always had a cheeky sentence in stock. Yet, on the inside she was like a wild, playful child — always a joke or a smile on her lips — and always behind the words was her natural honesty.

Though my visits to Elisabeth were short, and the tea no longer important — which was evidenced by the many other half-finished cups — each visit gave me so much more for my own life path. I appreciate the life she lived, and the importance of being real, authentic, honest, and doing what you truly love. Thank you, Bettli, for all you taught me. I love you forever. I remember you told me before you left your body, "If I leave my cocoon, I can be here for you even more."

Susan Bacher, Dr. Kübler-Ross's niece, is a craniosacral therapist who also teaches dance, yoga, and gymnastics. She resides in Basel, Switzerland, and travels often to India to study yoga and to Hawaii to swim with the dolphins.

The Swiss Hillbilly

By Rick Hurst

Elisabeth's life was spent traversing the world to bring her message
to those in need. The friends she made along the way remained loyal
and attentive to her throughout her life.

I met Elisabeth in the fall of 1984 at a workshop given by author
Ken Carey at his farm near St. Louis, Missouri. But it was at the
airport on our trip home that we began our 20-year friendship. The
agent at the airline desk looked at our tickets, then at us, and said,
"Wow. This is weird. You're Dr. Kübler-Ross, who wrote *On Death
and Dying,* and you're Cletus from *The Dukes of Hazzard.* What in the
world are you two doing together?"

Elisabeth quickly replied, "We belong together! I'm a hillbilly too
— a Swiss hillbilly!"

While Elisabeth's original plan was to be a country doctor, her practice expanded until it changed the medical model of Western civiliza-
tion. I was privileged to be a part of her life and to witness her unique
contribution of perseverance and determination, and her thirst for

truth, which revealed what was possible when those qualities were combined with unconditional love.

Of the many wonderful experiences I had with Elisabeth over the years, one of my favorite memories is the party for her birthday in 1998. She decided it was time to say goodbye to the "old" Elisabeth, the one who for a long time, cursed God in six languages over her stroke and the resulting diminished state, and to say hello to the "new," accepting Elisabeth.

So on a beautiful Saturday afternoon, a couple dozen friends and family members gathered around the teepee and totem pole in front of her Scottsdale home. We proceeded to have a Native American wake, complete with peace pipe ("A *r-r-real* one ... no phony baloney," she insisted), which the entire circle was obliged to enjoy. I think even the Buddhist priest had a puff. After songs, poems, and, naturally, the release of many brightly colored balloons, we moved inside for the celebration portion of the birthday party.

What happened next took me completely by surprise. Elisabeth motioned for me to come across the room to where she was sitting in her wheelchair. "Will you dance with me, please?" she asked. Rather stunned, since she had not been able to even use the walker for some time, I replied, "Sure ... but how?" She said, "I'll stand on top of your feet."

The next thing I knew Elisabeth and I were dancing around her living room to the "Tennessee Waltz!" Not to be outdone, all the other men at the party lined up and had their turn dancing with the birthday girl.

That day was a profound symbol of spirituality in practical application. Elisabeth ultimately was able to follow her own prescription, working through her anger and grief all the way to acceptance. She talked the talk and walked the walk. And, in this case, she danced the dance.

It was obvious to those of us who knew her and recognized her courage and commitment why she had emerged as a seminal figure and taken on not only the most pervasive taboo known to man — death — but also the most elusive of all subjects — life after death. She used her own intuition and the tools at hand to address the largest of questions. Who but Elisabeth would consider a dying patient a resource?

At a time on our planet when mankind is struggling to find compassion, understanding, and tolerance, it is only appropriate to recognize those who have enriched us all by employing these virtues in their life and work.

Today, thanks largely to Elisabeth, we have hospices and grief counseling programs throughout our nation. We have an entirely new field of medicine, thanatology, dedicated to the care of the terminally ill and those around them.

For these wonders and so many more, I'm pleased to have this opportunity to say thank you, Elisabeth, my friend, inspiration, and favorite Swiss hillbilly.

Rick Hurst was a longtime friend of Elisabeth's. As an actor, his film credits include *Steel Magnolias, M*A*S*H,* and *Anywhere But Here*. He has also starred in three television series, and is widely known for his role as Deputy Cletus Hogg in the TV series *The Dukes of Hazzard*. He is currently developing a movie for television based on the life of Elisabeth Kübler-Ross.

A Broken Pine Bough

By Joan Halifax Roshi

Joan Halifax Roshi, Buddhist teacher, Zen priest, and a fellow worker in the field of death and dying, was drawn to Elisabeth as a seeker of authenticity and truth. They shared a life approach that encompassed many levels of consciousness.

In the early 1980s, Elisabeth came to Santa Barbara, California, to give a talk for the Ojai Foundation. She was thin and personified high energy. She insisted on meeting everyone who wanted to spend time with her. I was concerned. She looked so tired. Her eyes were bloodshot. Her hands seemed to be tapping air. Her small body appeared to never rest. A bundle of coiled power with a mind like a great trap for suffering, she seemed to have only one purpose in life and had to fulfill it — and only it. She allowed nothing to get in her way.

Her talk was riveting, filled with stories of victories and losses. Her passion was obvious. Her mission was clear. She was going to change the face of death in America, and she was doing it, person by person. This was not a short talk; it went on for four powerful hours and was not about generalities, but dealt with the details of those lives that had touched and taught hers.

Somehow, in the course of her talk, she made many of us feel as though we had been in the presence of every dying person she mentioned. Though her physical presence was not large, her mind and heart created a magnetic field that was immense — that attracted what it needed to expand beyond her presence.

On our way to lunch, a small grey-colored man with deep shadows under his eyes grabbed Elisabeth's forearm and begged to speak with her. He was dying of lung cancer, he said, and there were some things he needed to know. Without a moment's hesitation, she invited him join us.

Clearly the lunch was about him. The rest of us sat quietly at the table as she queried him about his condition and his treatment, but mostly his state of mind. Her small salad was ignored as she smoked and listened. At times, the two of them seemed to be arguing. She was tough, straightforward, yet could be gentle. She did not let him hide behind any fact.

Despite the rigor of the exchange, the man began to visibly relax. His face seemed to get pinker as their conversation continued. And then it was over, and he skittered away.

Elisabeth looked around with relative disinterest at the small, mute group sitting at the table. She glanced at her salad with even less interest and abruptly invited us to finish up so we could go. A curtain of silence had fallen around her. She seemed both sad and angry. The story we had heard from our visitor with cancer revealed that this man had been in a medical wasteland. Less than a lunch's worth of attention had cracked opened his horizon.

In retrospect, I would call Elisabeth's compassion ruthless. Her priorities were clear, and she went straight for the truth — an arrow finding its target. She was brave, determined, and full of passion. She seemed dangerous if you had something to hide or were hiding behind a role, particularly a medical one.

I liked her, but never saw her again, to my regret. Yet the small taste of her presence 25 years ago touched me deeply, particularly her toughness sourced in love and compassion. There was no sugarcoating; in fact, there was no coating. Just this tough and magnificent woman who knew what she wanted and stopped at nothing to get it for others. She made no concessions in her courageous moves to uncover truth.

In Zen, we have a symbol that I feel captures her spirit. The broken pine bough brings together the truth of the relative aspects of existence with existence's eternal ultimate boundless expression — the truth of suffering and the absence of suffering, the truth of the phenomenal world and its emptiness of inherency and the truth of interconnectedness as well. Elisabeth seemed to live within the merging of the opposites.

She reconciled both extremes into compassionate action where the desire for an outcome drove her, and yet at the same time, she was not attached to the outcome.

She herself was a broken pine bough, something true, abiding, ancient in heart, and vulnerable.

Joan Halifax Roshi is founder, abbot, and head teacher of Upaya Zen Center, a Buddhist monastery in Santa Fe, New Mexico. Through the center, she is director of the project Being with Dying. A founding teacher of the Zen Peacemaker Order, she has focused her work for the last three decades on engaged Buddhism.

> *"All the hardships that*
> *come into our life are in*
> *reality gifts.*
> *They are opportunities*
> *to grow, which is the sole*
> *purpose of life."*

— Elisabeth Kübler-Ross, M.D.

Empress of Life

By Anneloes Eterman

Anneloes Eterman met Elisabeth only twice, but was inspired to devote her life to spreading her message via the Elisabeth Kübler-Ross Association in the Netherlands.

When I picture Elisabeth, I see her with black coffee and a cigarette instead of tea. That's in the days when she gave her Life, Death, and Transition workshops in the Netherlands. In the spring of 1982, just two months after I became the mother of my first child, Femke, I was blessed to attend such a workshop. It changed my life.

Until this day, I have committed myself to the Elisabeth Kübler-Ross group in the Netherlands, spreading the intellectual inheritance of Elisabeth Kübler-Ross. Some call her the Queen of Death, but to me, she is the Empress of Life.

I was very happy with my daughter, although I knew she would not live a long life. Femke was born with an open spine, and the doctors thought she'd probably die the same week. That week became one year.

Being a nurse, I had witnessed a lot of death and dying. The clumsy way most medical people treated a dying patient was annoying. When I was a student, I had read Elisabeth's books and her straightforward honesty was very appealing to me. She suggested that it could be done differently. I felt that as a challenge.

When I first saw Elisabeth, I hardly noticed her. Here was a small, gray-haired, simply dressed woman, nothing like a diva, nothing that indicated her worldwide fame. I thought I was attending some sort of seminar in which Elisabeth would give us lectures, and I would have to write things down like professional information and instructions. But it was not like that at all. It was experiential.

We all sat on mattresses on the floor. Elisabeth sat in a big chair, feet up, a thermos of black coffee and cigarettes on one side, and a cookie jar filled with tissues on the other.

I was shaking while explaining what brought me there. I started crying telling them about Femke. The first tissues had already been taken out of the jar for others, so I wasn't embarrassed.

Later she said, "Just draw anything," as she asked us to make spontaneous drawings. Some people were still rummaging about when suddenly we heard a piercing scream. The room became deadly silent. We were startled, and we thought someone was ill. It was only a participant unleashing a torrent of emotions. This was just the beginning of similar outbursts of emotions that would be released during the next three days. I didn't know a group could develop such a feeling of safety with each other in such a short period of time.

With the drawings in her lap, Elisabeth translated the symbolic language of the soul that was represented in them. It was surprising how much insight was to be gained from these simple drawings.

She also invited people to come forward to do specific release work on their life issues, and with every story told there were others who related to it and were touched by it. There were telephone books to be smashed with a rubber hose to help release the anger and suppressed emotions, and later a pillow to hug for comfort.

Elisabeth explained that to work with our unfinished business there is no right or wrong way. She gave us one clear instruction, though: "Do not try to comfort anybody by putting your arm around that person while he/she is still in the process of releasing the flow. That will stop it. If you do, I'll come and punch you in the face. Don't touch but stay in touch; give your attention but don't draw the attention to yourself; keep your mouth shut and just *be!* Simple."

While drinking coffee and chain-smoking, Elisabeth worked as a midwife. She was tough and patient, merciless but compassionate. It was obvious she believed in people and the power of love. She was determined to help us break through our own self-imposed barriers and allow the real person to emerge. She was humorous, and her self-esteem was astonishing. She knew what she was doing, and the work went on and on. I admire her deeply for the way she guided the flow.

Now she was the diva! I gave into the release of repressed feelings. I cried out anger and grief about all the wrong information I was given about life and love. My letting go was a relief. I felt no more shame or guilt.

My pain had nothing to do with the life of Femke, but because of her, I was drawn to Elisabeth, and found the way to *be* and let go.

According to Elisabeth, all the energy held within by repressed, depressed, and suppressed emotions was more frightening to her than the consciously invited expression of it. We listened to her comforting voice with that dear, funny, Swiss accent. I knew what she was teaching us wasn't about death and dying; it was about life and living!

In the following year, Elisabeth's wisdom was a great help in living with Femke and truly *being* there when she died, at home, surrounded by her loved ones. In spite of our grief, we were happy for Femke that she was free to leave the cocoon of her misshapen body. We treasure her life and will not forget: Death is not the end; it's just another form of life.

This philosophy helped us again when years later we lost our second child at birth, and it gave us the courage to welcome our wonderful healthy twins after that.

Elisabeth is my spiritual mother.

Although we met only twice, it was enough to cause me to dedicate my life to the message she brought to earth. She didn't want to be a guru or be placed on a pedestal. She considered herself simply a fellow human being and often said: "I'm not okay, you're not okay, and that's okay!"

I am proud to be a kindred spirit of such a blessed soul.

Anneloes Eterman is an art-drama therapist who specializes in working with spontaneous drawings. She has served as chairman of the board of directors of the Elisabeth Kübler-Ross Foundation, based in Zutphen, Netherlands, and also helped develop the hospice foundation there. She continues to write articles, lead workshops, and lecture on Elisabeth's work.

Learning to Live and Love Unconditionally

By Cheryl Shohan

A grieving mother and father are embraced into Elisabeth's life. The
mother finds her career path, and her family learns a
valuable life lesson.

I met Elisabeth 25 years ago at a San Francisco airport when she
was boarding an airplane. My husband Paul and I had two children. Our nine-year-old son had died six months before of aplastic
anemia, and our 13-year-old daughter had just been re-diagnosed
with bone cancer.

We had tried to see Elisabeth at a lecture nearby, but it was sold out
so we attempted to make contact with her at the airport. She wasn't
expecting us, and I didn't know what she looked like or the gate for
her flight. I walked into an area with many gates and hundreds of
people while Paul parked the car. I was befuddled. Just then, an old
friend came up to me and asked me to come meet her cousin.

Realizing I had no idea where to find Elisabeth, I followed my friend and was shaking her cousin's hand when I heard a voice with a Swiss accent. I recognized the voice from a cassette someone had slipped into my purse a few days before. A very small woman was standing two feet away in a parallel line. With my hand outstretched, I swiveled around and asked if she was Elisabeth Kübler-Ross.

I told her in a sentence or two about our situation, and she said, "Let's sit down while everyone boards the plane." She told us later she silently prayed to have more time with us, so she was the only one not surprised when it was announced over the loudspeaker that her flight was to be delayed for at least an hour.

We spent the next hour and a half sitting on the floor (there were no empty seats), talking, and smoking cigarettes. She invited my husband and me to her workshop, where she told me, "I will see you again and again and again."

A couple of months later our daughter, Kamala, would be the youngest participant to go to the workshops. Later, on the night Kamala died at home, Elisabeth's plane happened to be grounded because of fog, and she and Dr. Jerry Jampolsky and some other friends were with us in our tiny apartment.

Soon after, Elisabeth invited Paul and me to stay for a week at her home in Escondido, California, where she cooked and cared for us. I attended her training sessions, and Paul built a fence for her.

When we left, I felt lighter and penned a prophetic thank-you note saying, "Let's play together," which was to be a lot of our relationship for the next 20 years or more. We had fun together — silly, side-splitting, dissolve-into-laughter times together. We cooked and baked together, and we went shopping. You haven't shopped until you have gone shopping with Elisabeth! She never bought just one thing. There were bags and bags of everything.

It wasn't long before I realized my work in life was to be present for people facing life-threatening illness and death. I became a trainer and program director at the Center for Attitudinal Healing. I worked there for over 20 years with Jerry Jampolsky.

After Elisabeth's strokes, I would often stay with her in Arizona, usually for four or five days, sometimes a week or so. One night, there was what she called a "monsoon." There was a big leak in the roof and the rain was coming down so hard, it was like a waterfall 10 feet across in the middle of the house. Someone else was also visiting Elisabeth and together we found buckets and were trying to mop up the water. Elisabeth loved it. She was walking around and around with her walker marveling at her new indoor waterfall!

Now I don't want to make it sound like being with her was always just wonderful, because it wasn't. I would watch some people who came to help her leave the house completely frustrated with tears running down their cheeks, never to return again. I often wondered why in the world I put up with her. At times I felt like an indentured servant and at other times like an honored guest.

She could be such a martinet — giving orders, telling me to get this or that, or criticizing how I did things. Sometimes she told people who came to visit her how terrible I was, and she was unbelievably demanding at times.

I soon learned, however, that when I would put my foot down and stand up to her, there would always be a twinkle in her eye; I knew she loved that. She kept insisting that I needed to learn how to listen. So I watched her listen.

She continued to hold court and help the many people who were in need of her guidance and wisdom. Elisabeth gave love unconditionally, but not sentimentally.

As with so many others, my life changed because of Elisabeth. She helped me cope with my losses, and a subsequent cancer diagnosis, by being real and available. We had many profound spiritual conversations that I will always treasure.

One of my most fascinating memories of Elisabeth is of watching the various film crews that came to see her. She was never shy or intimidated. Instead, she seemed to take it as an opportunity to assist the individuals involved with their own life challenges. I watched as they arrived being very proper professionals, and noticed that when they left they looked brighter, as if being in touch with their own humanity had transformed them.

Anyone who really knew Elisabeth knows she never asked people to be different than they were, but she insisted they be authentic and genuine. She taught my family how to live life fully until we die.

So I spent the past 25 years of my life in a great adventure that included rounding up piglets on her farm in Virginia, feeding coyotes at her home in the desert, cooking, baking, arguing, loving, forgiving, and all the time learning from a master how to live and love unconditionally. I will love you always, Elisabeth.

Cheryl Shohan worked at the Center for Attitudinal Healing in Tiburon, California, with Gerald Jampolsky, M.D., for more than 20 years. She was co-founder of the Children with AIDS Program in San Francisco, California, and founder and director of the award-winning Home and Hospital Program, which offers services for the dying in the San Francisco Bay area. She lectures and conducts workshops throughout the United States, Latin America, Australia, and Western Europe, including the Findhorn Foundation in Scotland.

Living a Purpose-filled Life

By Joanne Cacciatore, Ph.D., L.M.S.W.

The grief over the death of her child brought Joanne to Elisabeth.
The inspiration, support, and wisdom she gained from Elisabeth
lifted her up and set her on her own unique life path.

I believe that my life has been touched by two of the most miraculous human beings who ever lived. One of them walked this
Earth only briefly. The other graced us with her wisdom and teachings for more than seven decades, soaring beyond expectations of any
cultural change that might come about in the single lifetime of one
mere mortal.

I remember it was a hot summer night in 1994. I had put my three
other children to bed and then sank onto the floor of my closet. I began
to sob helplessly, barely able to catch my breath. My arms ached and
every cell in my body longed to hold my precious daughter, Cheyenne,
who had died just a month earlier. I would sit on this closet floor repeating this agonizing scene for months.

There are no words to express the depth or magnitude of sorrow a parent feels after a child's death. Yet at the end of that year, after sinking into the abysmal and desperate grief of a bereaved mother, a kind and insightful soul offered me a book that would change my life forever. The book *On Children and Death* contained secret truths that gave me the light of hope during the darkest time of my life. A once-extinguished flame flickered in my heart, and I knew that one day, I would find my purpose.

Years later, I met Elisabeth, the woman whose words touched me and would further change my life. We bonded immediately, and I spent hours at a time getting to know this miracle of a person. There were times I was certain that she, like my little daughter who preceded her in death, was not of this Earth. That she was put here for a greater purpose, one of change and enlightenment, to teach compassion, kindness, and perspective.

Yet there were times that Elisabeth was just my friend — a "Swiss hillbilly" as her son, Ken, would affectionately call her. And my favorite part of the day was preparing English Breakfast tea and poached eggs for my very special friend. Elisabeth was the most genuine person I'd ever known. She was silly and demanding, sensitive and honest, playful and critical. But she was always authentic.

Sometimes we talked for hours. We talked about death, life, children, family, politics, and world events. She inspired me to pursue what she'd started with her work. Sometimes we would just sit in silence and watch the birds or the sunset. Sometimes words were not necessary with Elisabeth. In the silence, we knew one another's thoughts, fears, and pains.

Elisabeth's inspiration did give birth to my purpose, and thus, the MISS Foundation (Mothers in Sympathy and Support) came to be, an international non-profit organization I founded in 1996 that provides aid, support, and advocacy for grieving families after the death of an infant or young child. Today, the foundation has grown to more than 70 chapters and tens of thousands of members around the world, and so, the flicker of Elisabeth's candle has, again, lit countless other candles.

During the course of our friendship, there were times when I wanted to give up this work, disheartened by the never-ending sadness of child death. Elisabeth gently reminded me that I hadn't chosen this course. This course had, in fact, chosen me. "Continue, Joanne," she said. "You have to continue."

A few weeks before her death, I had a dream that Elisabeth died. In my dream, I was sobbing and mourning, feeling desperate to have my friend back. She appeared to me, surprised by my sadness. She told me to stop crying and assured me that she was fine. Then she told me not to worry, well aware of my enduring tug-of-war with faith. She said reassuringly, "I'll see you again one day."

When I visited Elisabeth the next day, I told her that I dreamed about her the previous night.

She asked, "Was it a good dream?"

I replied hesitantly, "Well, not really."

She asked further, "Did I die?"

"Yes," I said, looking down.

Elisabeth told me that she was waiting for death to come so she could do all the things that her broken body could no longer do. She assured me that when she died, she could help me more with my work from the other side than she could here. I walked away from our conversation that day knowing that when the time came, it would be very hard to say goodbye, yet I realized that she would never *really* leave any of us; her work would never end.

I came home the night of Elisabeth's funeral service exhausted and aching. I already missed her so much and felt grief's grip around my chest. Around 11 p.m. I went outside onto my front patio and sat in my rocking chair. I leaned my head back and began to sob, talking to Elisabeth in my mind. With tears rolling down my cheeks, I asked her for a sign, for a very clear sign. I asked her for something like a shooting star, not really expecting anything miraculous.

A few minutes later, I opened my eyes and immediately saw a bright shooting star traveling from the east to the west. And for that, I was grateful. I realized that Elisabeth is, indeed, doing what she said she would be doing. She is busy guiding and inspiring us all, dancing and singing and playing amongst the galaxies, surrounded by stars.

Never forget Elisabeth's timeless words: "Dying is nothing to fear. It can be the most wonderful experience of your life. It all depends on how you have lived."

And so, the legacy of Dr. Elisabeth Kübler-Ross will live on. Tell your children, grandchildren, and great-grandchildren about this truly miraculous human being who was able to transform the way the world thought about death and dying. She is truly now one who soars.

Joanne Cacciatore is a certified thanatologist and grief counselor skilled in the area of parental bereavement. She founded the MISS Foundation, an international non-profit organization that provides aid, support, and advocacy for grieving families after the death of an infant or young child. She is the author of four books, including *Dear Cheyenne*, which is in its sixth printing.

Cherishing a Baby's Brief Life

By Amy Kuebelbeck

Drawn to Elisabeth's writings as a teenager, Amy Kuebelbeck began
unknowingly storing valuable information that would help her survive
her worst grief, the death of her newborn son.

L ike millions of others around the world, I consider Elisabeth
Kübler-Ross among my greatest teachers, although we never met.
My classroom with Elisabeth was my childhood home in the woods of
Minnesota, where as a teenager I curled up with her books and became
enthralled by her transcendent messages: Death is not to be feared. Death
has meaning. And, most luminous of all: Death is not the end.

Many have discovered her writings following the death of someone
they love, as they sought and then found wisdom and comfort in her
words. For me, her insights gently helped lay a foundation that would
help me years later to embrace the brief life of my newborn son.

Elisabeth was a trailblazer not only for those nearing the end of a
long life. She also recognized that radical change was needed when

death comes at the beginning of life. Although the death of a baby before or after birth is not uncommon, for decades it was shrouded in silence.

Parents typically were not allowed to see their dead baby and were advised to forget about it and have another one. Babies' bodies were often buried hastily, sometimes in unmarked common graves, while the mother was still recuperating in the hospital. Even today, bodies sometimes are unceremoniously incinerated along with hospitals' medical waste. Too often, these babies are never spoken of again.

Elisabeth touched on this in her book *On Children and Death* and in a deeply moving 1986 video titled *Some Babies Die* in which she said:

> "Our present Western society is not willing to experience death, in the sense that it is hidden by a conspiracy of silence. The sudden and unexplained death of a baby is very tragic, yet it is not regarded as something to be sad over, especially if the baby has never lived. As a consequence, parents are often not given permission by family or friends to mourn the death of their baby, and they are very often left alone in an apparently unsympathetic world, not knowing how to feel and not knowing how to cope."

Her pioneering work in death and dying helped pave the way for a significant cultural shift in which parents were being given permission to mourn the death of a baby. Driven by persistent efforts of bereaved parents, many hospitals have adopted more compassionate practices. Instead of being admonished to forget about the baby, parents often are now encouraged to see and hold their baby, honoring parents' instincts of tenderness and love. They are invited to create memories: to give their baby a name, to collect handprints and footprints, and to take photographs.

These parents will not be leaving the hospital with a baby, but unlike far too many heartbroken mothers and fathers in the past, they will at least be recognized as parents of a unique, irreplaceable child.

I believe Elisabeth's work will also help light the path for a new phenomenon, one being created by medical advances that didn't exist when she first began to insist that those who are dying are worth our attention and care. Today, terminal conditions are being diagnosed before a baby is even born.

I have traveled this path myself. I was five-and-one-half months pregnant when my husband and I learned that our son, Gabriel, had an incurable heart condition. Despite some wrenchingly aggressive surgical options, no one could give our son a good heart. So we set out to give him a good, although brief, life. What ensued was an extraordinary journey of grief, joy, and love as we waited with Gabriel. Much of what we did was in the spirit of hospice and in the spirit of Elisabeth's famous urging to "live until you die."

During that gift of time, we prepared for his birth, prepared for his death, and embraced his life. We involved his two young sisters, many family members, and friends. Our baby lived for nine months before he was born and for two-and-one-half peaceful hours afterward.

During his gentle transition from life to death, he was cradled by my husband and me, surrounded by a roomful of people who loved him. As we inscribed on his gravestone, "He knew only love."

In too many places, the ability to diagnose fatal conditions prenatally has raced ahead of the ability to care for these families and their babies. But in a beautiful and practical response, a response made possible by Elisabeth's lifetime of work, some hospitals and hospices around the world are starting to use a perinatal hospice approach to help these families give their babies — and themselves — the gift of a loving welcome and a peaceful goodbye.

These parents need and deserve holistic support to embrace the profound privilege of pouring out a lifetime of love in a few sacred days, hours, or moments. This new way of thinking is a logical outgrowth of Elisabeth's work, which will continue to bear fruit in new and unexpected ways for years to come.

In part because of Elisabeth, parents like me have memories of our babies to sustain us, as well as permission from others to grieve and remember. Because I can look at photographs of my son, graze my fingers across his plaster-of-Paris footprints, or breathe in the faint fragrance of hospital soap that lingers on the one soft cotton outfit I was able to dress him in, I know that I owe Elisabeth a debt of gratitude.

She said that after she died, "I'm going to dance first in all the galaxies." So Elisabeth, if you are not too busy, could you please take the hand of my little boy and take him dancing with you in one of your favorite galaxies?

Amy Kuebelbeck is one of the millions of people around the world who were touched and helped by the work of Elisabeth Kübler-Ross. She is the author of *Waiting With Gabriel: A Story of Cherishing a Baby's Brief Life*, a poignant book, which was also published in Italy as *Aspettando Gabriel*.

The Pain and Healing of Grief

By Carol Kearns, Ph.D.

Elisabeth's counsel and compassion unlock a mother's grief and
lead her to a life of service to other bereaved parents.

Before my first meeting with Elisabeth in 1976, I had great concern about what she would say to me. She was speaking in Medford, Oregon, and friends had arranged for me to meet privately with her after the lecture.

My seven-year-old daughter, Kristen, had died one month earlier while we were vacationing on the Oregon coast. A freak wave had pulled her out to sea.

I was fearful that this expert on death and dying would somehow force me to accept Kristen's death, and I wasn't ready. I was still in what she would describe as the first stage of grief — shock and denial. The Coast Guard had recovered my daughter's body 10 days after she drowned, and I was not allowed to see her because of the condition of the body. I was functioning on two different levels of reality: one where I believed she was dead and another where I refused to accept it.

When we arrived for Elisabeth's day-long lecture, the auditorium was packed. Soon a small figure appeared on stage in Birkenstock sandals and a simple Indian-style dress. She was so tiny that when she stood behind the lectern, she almost disappeared. Someone gave her a hand-held microphone, and she walked over to a table, perched herself on the edge, and sat casually swinging her legs. She began to speak softly in a Swiss accent. In this auditorium of hundreds, you could have heard a pin drop. I wondered how I could have been afraid of this person.

During her lecture she read poems written by bereaved parents who addressed feelings I had but was incapable of expressing. The painful words of these grieving parents chipped away at the last remnants of my denial, and by the time I met with Elisabeth, I was an emotional wreck. Taking my hands in hers, she gently pulled me to the side of the room away from the crowd. Elisabeth lovingly held me as I allowed the tears to flow. This was the beginning of a long and wonderful relationship.

My experience in this first meeting was comforting. She didn't give me answers as I had feared, but she did arouse in me feelings that were powerful and foreign. I especially remember the issue of anger, an emotion I was not conscious of at the time. As I discovered later in my grief work, it was devouring me. I was surprised when she asked me what I had done with my anger. "I don't feel angry," I answered. "I just feel sad and frightened. I can't live without Kristen and don't know how to help my 10-year-old son Michel." She calmly replied, "Unless you wanted this to happen, you are probably going to feel some anger."

Once I worked through my own grief, I wanted to help others in crisis, especially bereaved parents. Elisabeth was supportive. She understood the power of the bond that creates a lifeline of hope among grieving parents. I had been discouraged by other medical professionals who believed my working with bereaved parents would be too painful for me to be effective.

Elisabeth continued to encourage me and invited me to Shanti Nilaya, her healing center located in the hills of Escondido, California. I was doing my own grief work, as well as assisting in her workshops, working in the kitchen, planting tulips, answering mail, and helping in any way needed.

After four months, I talked to her about leaving to be closer to my son, Michel, who was living in Oregon with his father. I loved working with her but realized I was not only grieving for Kristen, but also for my son who was very much alive and whom I missed dearly.

She supported my need to be near Michel, and she also suggested I write a book as a way to reach out and help other people. Not being a writer, I have spent years working on the book and am finally close to completing it. Whenever I saw her, she would ask me about the book. I would guiltily reply that I was still working on it. She once said, "I don't think I'll live to see the day it's completed." Sadly she was right.

In her unique way, Elisabeth helped me to find myself again. I realized early that Kristen's death would either be the greatest growth experience of my life, or it would destroy me. Elisabeth guided me through my grief, and encouraged me to return to school and get my degree in order to counsel others in pain. Her support and belief in me is the reason I became a psychologist, giving purpose to my pain and instilling new meaning to my life.

Fearlessly, Elisabeth ventured where no one else dared. Only the strokes she suffered later in her life slowed her down. I was honored then to help her at a most difficult time. Finally, I had a chance to repay her for "saving" my life.

The last years were difficult for Elisabeth. She raged against a body that failed her when she longed to be active. She was disabled in a way that left her unable to cook, knit, and garden, some of her favorite pastimes. Caring for her was challenging. Anyone caught in the crossfire of her frustration was likely to become the next victim of her anger. For a woman who enjoyed being in control, disability was the cruelest of punishments.

I miss Elisabeth. My relationship with her had always been a private one, and I liked it that way. I will treasure the many conversations we shared over the past 30 years. At her memorial service I was not feeling sad, but rather joyful for Elisabeth. She was now free of her broken body and able to dance in the galaxy as she wished. This image makes me smile.

Dr. Carol Kearns retired after 25 years in private practice as a clinical psychologist in San Francisco. She was active with The Compassionate Friends, an international organization of bereaved parents, as well as other Bay Area bereaved parent organizations.

> *"There are no accidents;*
> *everything in life happens for a*
> *positive reason."*
>
> — Elisabeth Kübler-Ross, M.D.

The French Connection

By Hervé Mignot, M.D.

Hervé Mignot was expecting a formal meeting with an international
icon in an antiseptic medical setting. What he got was classic
Elisabeth: home cooking, lodging, and the opportunity of a lifetime.

The first time I met Elisabeth Kübler-Ross was in 1991. She was
already internationally known for her enormous contribution
to terminally ill patients, and I had read all of her books. As a French
physician recently involved in palliative care, I had dreamed of meeting her. I wanted to tell her how much her books had helped me on a
professional and personal level.

I was in Canada for a professional survey of different palliative care
units. She was headquartered in an area on the East Coast of the U.S. So,
in spite of my colleagues telling me that her time was always overbooked
and she was a little bit mad, I sent a fax to Angie, her secretary, to apply
for an appointment. The answer was positive — such a big, wonderful surprise!

All my Canadian friends asked me to tell them later how she was and if it was true that she had lost her cleverness due to her health challenges.

I decided to fly in the day before my appointment. Naturally I took a jacket and a tie, as one is to do when you are to meet one of your medical professors. I had no U.S. dollars. I planned to find a hotel, to look for currency, and to rent a car to be able to reach her office, which I believed was two hours away from the airport in Shenandoah Valley, Virginia.

During the flight I practiced what I would say to her to express my acknowledgment of her life and work. I changed planes many times from Montreal to the final airport, which was so small I couldn't find a bank or a rental car.

I had travelled in jeans and a tee shirt, expecting to change into a shirt and tie for my appointment with Elisabeth the following day. As I walked across the tarmac, I noticed an old Indian man, with a strong face, sitting nearby. He said to me, "You're coming to see Elisabeth, I guess. I can drive you if you want."

I was so ashamed to disturb her, as I had arrived a day early, and was wearing such casual clothes. I told him no, but he had already called Angie, who said, "Let him come."

I felt like an idiot as we arrived at the farm and was immediately surrounded by two big Saint Bernard dogs. Elisabeth came down from her little house on top of the hill. She looked at me, pushed me into the kitchen, and said, "You've made a long trip; you may be hungry; do you want an egg?"

I felt stupid and was unable to say any of my prepared speech. She started to open drawers and cupboards and to cook different dishes. I was forced to eat the first one, and when she finished her work, she sat straight in front of me and asked, "Why are you here?"

I was shocked. I had imagined being received in a formal office in a hospital with doctors and nurses, and here I was in strange surroundings in the middle of nowhere. I suddenly realized that I believed she was able to read in my heart the sadness and the overwhelming desire I had to slink out of her presence and to die. I stood up and said, "I just want to say thank you for your work that has changed my life. Now, I can leave."

She pushed me back on my chair and said, "Tell me about your life; why don't you share that with me?" I told her of my family and personal story, about how I was a fifth-generation physician, but was unable to become a professor of medicine like my predecessors.

I told her that I had been involved for many years with Doctors of the World in Afghanistan, Senegal, South Africa, Chad, and Lebanon. I shared with her that I had a strong desire to bring more humanity and brotherhood to those who are facing adversity and death.

I complained that there was no Elisabeth Kübler-Ross group in France like in other countries and asked her why.

She listened to me carefully and asked me to stay with her. She showed me to my room, and gave me towels and soap. She told me that I could be the one who could build the group in France.

She called Angie to register me for the next workshops in America and in Europe. "Don't worry," she said, "you will be able to do it if you really want it."

I spent five days with Elisabeth that I would never forget. She explained to me how she came to help people face death. She shared with me her professional and spiritual experiences.

I realized I had found a kindred spirit, a guide for my life path. I worked hard on my "unfinished business" during many workshops. I was the only French man in attendance.

I came back to the farm many times in the 1990s, and I remember one Christmas weekend in particular. Elisabeth had erected a true Christmas tree in her living room with real candles. With an old friend, a New York dentist, we spent the night singing and celebrating the birth of Christ.

Back in France, I started to meet people who were interested in Elisabeth's work. I had been trained to organize workshops, and we did that. We also created individual and mutual support groups for people in grief. We delivered information and training.

Elisabeth called me in February 1994. She was ready to come to Paris for a lecture in April. We had only two months to prepare a conference. Nearly 1,500 people came to it, which was almost as many as for a previous lecture by the Dalaï Lama.

At the beginning of our work in France and throughout Europe, medical professionals were very critical of this new group and its teachings. Elisabeth was not highly esteemed in Europe because of her spiritual beliefs. I felt this discrimination also, but little by little, year after year, this began to dissipate.

As the European Association of Palliative Care (EAPC) organized its congress 100 days before the year 2000, I was asked to interview her. The scientific committee wanted to honour the two pioneers of palliative care in the world: Dame Cicely Saunders and Elisabeth Kübler-Ross.

I came to her new house in Arizona to videotape an interview with her. I found her tired and handicapped by several strokes, but so human. She was just like any other old woman, the opposite of a guru! Yet as soon as she faced the camera, she once again found her energy source, a beautiful light came into her eyes, and she started to speak like before, giving us her testimony for the future.

In the video she reiterated the tender, loving philosophy that was the hallmark of her lifework. The clarity, truth, and presence of this great soul, as well as the wisdom she shared were obvious and powerful. The homage the EAPC congress paid to her at the event was unanimous.

When I learned she had died, I remembered what she had taught me: You better tell cherished people you love them rather than waiting to buy flowers for their funeral. As I had many opportunities to tell her of my love for her, I began to seek one good reason to come to Arizona for the ceremony.

I subsequently received a call from her son, Ken Ross, and then from many other people throughout Europe. I was called to represent them and to deliver messages to her family. Ken asked me to officially represent the scientific community at the funeral.

Through me, I felt that this old Europe would, at last, be able to express its recognition of Elisabeth's life and work. I couldn't let the opportunity pass.

At the service in Arizona, I read the official declarations of the French and European Associations of Palliative Care, the French Society of Thanatology, the French Elisabeth Kübler-Ross Association, and many others. Through their collective expressions of gratitude and tributes for her pioneering work in promoting the hospice movement, and her incredible lifelong commitment to the terminally ill and their families, her contributions were fully acknowledged.

Then I let my prepared remarks go and said: I just want to say thank you, Elisabeth, for the blessing that has been our friendship, and also to point out your tremendous gift to the medical profession.

Through your work, we have been able to pay more attention to physical, psychological, and spiritual sufferance of the terminally ill patients. We have been less terrified by death, which as you taught us, is a natural

151

experience. The description of the psychological pathway of dying has been the beginning of an international movement, which goes on.

Would that we never let our humanity forget that despite the struggle for life and the fear of death, we are made for love. God bless you, Elisabeth.

Dr. Hervé Mignot was the force behind the palliative care movement in France. He founded the Elisabeth Kübler-Ross Association there in 1993 and continues as its president. He teaches palliative care and grief support at the Universities of Paris and Tours.

Coincidence or Cosmic Dance?

By Robert Singleton

Embraced in the loving dynamic of Elisabeth's workshop, a soul is
freed to come out and accept who he truly is and to assist
his friends as they seek a peaceful death.

In the early 1980s, a friend handed me a magazine article about a
remarkable, enlightened woman named Elisabeth Kübler-Ross. I
was greatly moved by her words, so I remembered her name.

In 1986, a radio reporter friend welcomed me as a tagalong when he
went to interview Elisabeth at her home. We ended up spending the
entire day in her Virginia kitchen talking, laughing, and eating the
wonderful food she prepared.

By rural standards, we were practically neighbors, and I wanted to
return Elisabeth's hospitality, so as I was leaving I invited her to my home
to see my paintings. I presumed she was quite busy, and I left with no
expectation that I'd hear from her anytime soon.

A week later, to my surprise, Elisabeth called and said she'd like to take me up on my invitation. On February 22, 1986, just as a heavy snow started to fall, she arrived at my front door with a friend.

After dinner we went into the studio for a presentation of my recent works. As I displayed the paintings one at a time, I explained them this way: "These are simply a documentation of my own journey toward the light. You'll notice that in each the source of the light is slightly obscured, just out of sight. With each successive painting you seem to be moving closer to the source of the light — yet the source is never revealed."

Elisabeth asked if I would ever paint the source of the light, and I answered. "Oh no! I don't think I'm good enough to paint the source of the light. Hopefully I'll see it when I die." Elisabeth said no more to me about the subject.

By the time I'd shown all the paintings, it was snowing quite heavily, and I urged my guests to spend the night. Later that evening, Elisabeth's friend came to me in private and repeated what Elisabeth had said to him: "You know, it's amazing, he has already seen the light and doesn't even know it. The light is in all of his work."

The next morning, as they prepared to leave, Elisabeth invited me to come as her guest to one of her Life, Death, and Transition workshops. She said, "I want you to see the work I do."

Arrangements were made, and I attended the five-day workshop. The intensity of Elisabeth's work was life-altering for me. What a catharsis!

I "came out" publicly in front of 100 people. Previously, this act would have required panicky courage. However, in an atmosphere of unconditional love and safety, a dynamic was created for me to share openly that denied part of who I am. One hundred people compassionately and unconditionally accepted me as a human being, and through that unconditional love, I learned to accept myself.

Finally, after nearly 50 years of denial, my sexuality was no longer an issue for me. I was freed to be myself with no condemnation. I was spiritually healed. I owe all of this — singularly — to Dr. Elisabeth Kübler-Ross.

Elisabeth soon invited me to join the board of directors for the Elisabeth Kübler-Ross Center, and I served until the center's 1995 closing. During those years I got to know this exceptional human being as a colleague and personal friend. I grew increasingly protective of her name and her mission for humanity, and I was careful never to take advantage of this privileged friendship, nor to burden her with my personal problems. However, on three occasions I specifically asked for her wisdom and comfort. In each case, it was out of love for a lifelong friend who was nearing death from AIDS.

Elisabeth always responded. Amidst her busy schedule, traveling worldwide, she stopped being Dr. Ross, and as if she were an old friend, called my ailing loved ones. I witnessed those conversations and saw my friends' faces light up. Despite never having met her, they spoke to her with such ease, and they smiled as if sharing a secret. She knew them and knew their journey quite beyond mortal understanding.

Many of Elisabeth's teachings have become integrated into the everyday life and lexicon of this culture. Her personal authorship of this wisdom seems to have been lost along the way, her genius plagiarized on too many occasions. Yet, I suspect, if I were able to tell her of my concern, the consternation on my face would be met with a wry and knowing smile on hers.

Elisabeth came into my life at a fateful moment. She awakened me to self-love, and out of that came the strength and insight to assist others in finding not only their own source of infinite love but also the peace to make their transition.

I've covered a mountainside on my property with the ashes of too many of my friends lost to this disease known as AIDS. It is my honor to provide them a resting place away from a world that judged them so unfairly.

Because Elisabeth helped me find my own strength and the courage to accept myself, I could be there for them on their last journey. I thank her for allowing me to give her and her loving counsel as a grace-filled final gift to those loved ones.

Some might say I met Dr. Elisabeth Kübler Ross by chance. I don't think so. AIDS was about to become an epidemic, and many soldiers would step forth, with Elisabeth leading the battle against rampant ignorance and prejudice. As I heard Elisabeth say many times, "There is no such thing as coincidence." With all my heart I believe we met by means of a cosmic, sacred dance, choreographed long before we knew each other's names.

Robert Singleton is internationally acclaimed for his artwork featuring spiritual light. His work is represented in prestigious private and public collections. In 1995 he founded Russell House, a sanctuary for those living with HIV/AIDS and for those who care for them.

How I Met Elisabeth the First Time

By Tom Hockemeyer

This was definitely a publisher-author-friend relationship destined to happen. Elisabeth could share her dark night of the soul and any supernatural experiences with this kindred spirit.

In 1983 while visiting a friend in Alabama, I read a magazine article titled *There is No Death* by Elisabeth Kübler-Ross. I knew instantly that I had to meet this Swiss doctor.

After locating her in Southern California, I phoned and was invited to attend the last evening of one of her famous, five-day workshops.

Driving a rental car, I found the beautiful, remote retreat amidst big sandstone boulders and pine trees in the surroundings of Escondido. The group of about 70 workshop participants had just completed their evening meal.

I asked for Elisabeth and was told that she was gone and nobody knew where. A short time later a pickup drove in and there she was sitting on the bed of the truck, which was filled with collected pinecones for the ceremony that was to follow.

I approached her and told her that I was the invited guest from Germany. She called on a German Sikh with a beard and a white turban and told him, "Tell Tom what it's all about here."

At the pinecone ceremony each of the participants, some in wheelchairs, took a pinecone and, following instructions, filled it verbally with everything from which they desired to be free. With this new decision for a changed life, they then threw the pinecones into the blazing fire.

Elisabeth then called on the five Swiss and German people in the group to step forward by the fire where we placed our arms on each others shoulders — with Elisabeth in the middle — and sang "Guten Abend, gute Nacht," the famous lullaby.

By this time it was nearly midnight, and a man from Switzerland and I went with Elisabeth on an unforgettable walk under the full moon. We were talking about spirit guides. She had a personal spirit guide who showed up once in a while or talked to her.

She related this story. On one occasion she was in Australia on a lecture and seminar tour. She was in her hotel room and became deeply depressed about such thoughts as: "What kind of life do I have? I am racing from one country to another, from one auditorium to another, from one hotel room to another. I have no personal life. Why am I doing all of this? I want to stop this way of life. I want to give up."

While she was sobbing, all of a sudden her spirit guide materialized his upper body right in front of her. He smiled at her, stretching out his arm and touching her gently on the back of her neck with his hand. She felt an energy flowing right though her neck into her whole body. When her guide dematerialized, the depression was gone. She promised: "I will go on with my work! No matter what the struggles or hardships, it doesn't matter!"

The many times we were together, we were talking about the unseen friends who had helped her in a tremendous way throughout her life. And often when she got proof of their help, she would raise her right arm up high and say thank you, then kiss her right forefinger and blow a kiss to them.

At that time, I did not know that I was to become the German publisher for all her spiritual books, culminating in her most famous book, *About Death and the Life Hereafter*.

She told me that her real mission in life was to leave people these messages: There is no death. We will continue to live after leaving our earthly body. We will further exist in the spirit world until we reincarnate in the womb of a new mother.

Tom Hockemeyer is co-founder of the German publishing house Silberschnur Verlag. He published five German editions of Elisabeth's books, and subsequently became a lifelong friend. He is a well-known novelist writing under the pseudonym Trutz Hardo, as well as an author of books on reincarnation and the laws of karma. He studied reincarnation and past-life regression with Richard Sutphen, and is now one of Germany's most widely known regressionists. He is a much sought-after lecturer on spiritual and esoteric subjects.

Elisabeth's Japan Connection

By Ryoko Dozono, M.D.

Dr. Dozono was drawn to the life and work of Dr. Kübler-Ross, and after several meetings with her, established the Elisabeth Kübler-Ross Center in Tokyo.

Two of my passports — one issued in 1993 and the other in 1998 — are visual reminders of my association with Elisabeth. They bear witness to my success in finally getting to meet her after several previous attempts, beginning in 1995, had failed.

My first successful meeting with Elisabeth occurred in 1999 when I took a taxi from Phoenix Sky Harbor International Airport to her home in Scottsdale, Arizona. It was exactly as she described in her book: the wooden gate, the Native American teepee, and the Swiss flag waving a friendly greeting from the top of the house.

I knocked on the door and heard a voice say, "Come in." I opened the door gently and stepped into the house. It was dark and quiet inside. Again I heard the voice from the far side of the house say, "Come in." As

I walked toward the voice, I saw her. She was sitting in her armchair next to a large window that bathed her in brilliant sunshine.

I walked up close to her, and as I did, she extended the index finger of her right hand to reach me, and I touched it with mine just like the E.T. greeting in the movie.

I soon realized we were alone in the house. She said almost immediately, "Go to the kitchen and make yourself a cup of tea."

This was the beginning of my *Tea with Elisabeth* encounters. I cannot recall the many times afterward that I had tea with Elisabeth. I do know that we took tea together at her Scottsdale home, at her son's house, and in the group home where she eventually took leave of the earth as an eagle or butterfly.

Actually, now that I am reliving those times, I remember we often had wine or saké instead of tea, particularly on the special occasion of her or her son's birthday.

I believe because of the heart connection we had, we were also able to communicate telepathically. The conversations we did share were deep, meaningful, and filled with inspiration.

In 2002, I visited her with my daughter Kei (pronounced Kay). Elisabeth's advice to her was short, crisp, and simple: "Do not listen to your mother!" Elisabeth was right, as Kei was 20 years old and already independent.

Elisabeth's thoughts are always in my mind, and her voice is everpresent in my ear. Among the wise thoughts she imparted to me, two are unforgettable and give me great sustenance when I am going through hard times. They are: "Everything happens for a reason," and "Do not place expectations on others."

I also loved hearing her repeat her favorite pronouncement, "Naturally!" This was usually presented with great enjoyment by Elisabeth, as it represented her wise acknowledgment of a fellow soul's newly discovered and enhanced understanding of a universal truth.

I had never thought about establishing an Elisabeth Kübler-Ross Center in Japan; all I wanted and dreamed about was just getting to meet her. Yet here I am 10 years after I first began seeking a meeting with her. I am sitting in the Tokyo office of the Elisabeth Kübler-Ross Center and remembering and thinking about the wonderful influence she has had on my life.

I know if I could tell her that it was my fate to meet her so that I could share her life and philosophy with so many others at this center in Tokyo, she would say, "Naturally!"

I look forward to having tea with her again!

Dr. Ryoko Dozono was born in Tokyo and graduated from Keio University School of Medicine in 1971. From 1977-1980 she was a research fellow at the University of Southern California School of Medicine. In 1984 she started the International Medicine Crossing Office, which combined Oriental and Western medicine. In 2001 she established the Elisabeth Kübler-Ross Center, Japan Chapter, which is headquartered in her medical offices.

Remembering the Joy in a Life Well Lived

By Gerald Jampolsky, M.D., and Diane Cirincione, Ph.D.

Longtime friends and colleagues remember the good times, and
honor Elisabeth's life and work by continuing to further her universal
message by incorporating it into their philosophy and their
professional lives.

E lisabeth, to "take tea" with you once again through the pages of
this book is very special for us. You hold a cherished place in
our hearts and are eternally very much alive. It seems as if we have
known each other forever.

I remember the first time you met my wife, Diane. You were lecturing in Palo Alto, California, and I was lecturing in San Francisco
the same night. I had purchased the special Swiss chocolates that you
loved so much and asked Diane to give them to you before you presented your lecture. Diane asked how she would know you, and I
remember saying, "Just trust … you will know."

That night before the performance Diane went to the restroom. As
she entered, a woman was coming out of one of the stalls. Diane said,

"Are you Elisabeth?" And your response was, in your typical sharp fashion, "Oh my God, they will find me wherever I am!"

Luckily, Elisabeth, you then saw the chocolates and said, "Oh, I bet Jerry sent those to me."

Throughout the many years Diane and I have known you, we have so many precious memories of being with and learning from you.

You were the teacher "par excellence" as you modeled being fearless by being the greatest giraffe of all, sticking your neck out farther than anyone we knew. You made it clear that you were not in this life to win a popularity contest. Your compassion and ability to help others was incomparable.

We are two of the lucky ones who got to spend time with you as you cooked and laughed, talked about your guides, and did your best to live your life to the fullest. Even in those last years that you were here on the physical plane, confined to a wheelchair much of the time, you taught us that a physical illness was not going to take the flame of life away from you.

We remember the night that the negative *Time* magazine article about you came out, and you saw it just before we went on stage. We thought you were going to blow the roof off with your anger, but you allowed us to play a part in defusing you.

We will never forget your collection of thimbles that was destroyed in the fire, and the numerous times you were called upon to deal with your own lessons involving stress and illness.

We have visited you in Virginia, San Diego, and Scottsdale, and your supercharged battery was always in effect no matter what personal crisis you were facing.

We love you dearly, Elisabeth, and carry your teaching and friendship with us always.

Dr. Gerald G. "Jerry" Jampolsky is an internationally recognized authority in the fields of psychiatry, health, and education. In 1975 he was the co-founder of the original Center for Attitudinal Healing in Tiburon, California, for children and adults with life-threatening illnesses. This model for support groups is now used extensively worldwide. A prolific writer, his books include *Love Is Letting Go of Fear, Goodbye to Guilt,* and *One Person Can Make a Difference.*

Dr. Diane V. Cirincione is a therapist as well as an internationally known lecturer and author. She wrote *Sounds of the Morning Sun* and co-authored six books with her husband, Dr. Jampolsky. She is co-founder with Barbara Marx Hubbard of *The Regenopause Dialogues,* which revalue and redefine the stages of women's lives.

The Eagle Has Flown to the Stars

By Elayne Reyna

Elayne and Elisabeth were two "eagles" who remembered their song,
and enjoyed singing and soaring together.

I am Bluebird. I am a bringer of song. My path of service is helping people remember their song. Life, in all its sweetness and
sorrow, evokes songs of celebration, honoring, joy, meditation, and
songs that pierce the heart to purge grief. When the song has gone far
beyond the distant star, I come to call it back and to wipe away tears. I
sing breath into the heart to live as a new song of courage and inner
peace.

Our life is our song. Early on, young Elisabeth knew her song.
Elisabeth's was a brave song of courage, humor, inspiration, joy, no-
bility, passion for life, and compassion for the dying.

Sometimes life makes us lose our song. As a young woman, I joined
the U.S. Air Force and was trained as a medic during wartime. Not

given counseling on how to process my feelings around the horror of dying young men and the futility of war, I lost my song.

In 1975, I read *On Death and Dying* and became deeply affected by Elisabeth's natural and supernatural understanding of what are, for me, the ancient, ancestral ways of honoring the dying with dignity and respect. I went to Connecticut College with my surgical team to see and hear this heroic woman's unforgettable lecture. Through the years, I entered ceremonies for soul retrieval and learned healing songs to help people.

When Elisabeth beckoned me to see her in Shenandoah, Virginia, I prayed on what I'd do that would be meaningful for her. I took my sacred things — my drum, my shawl, and my sacred pipe. And I took a song for Elisabeth.

Elisabeth gave me a deerskin tobacco pouch, and I placed a medicine shawl on her to honor and keep her strong for the work she was doing for the terminally ill. Elisabeth and I entered into a sacred relationship as ceremonially adopted sisters. I was blessed to have her as my Big Sister.

I asked, "Elisabeth, what is it you want me to do for you?'

Smiling broadly and rolling her r's, Elisabeth replied, "I like to dr-r-r-r-um!"

I asked, "Do you want me to teach you to drum?"

With a great smile and bright eyes, she proudly voiced, "No, Bluebird. I have my own drumbeat. I just want you and me to dr-r-r-rum!"

And so, we dr-r-r-rummed! And we sang! And with every heartbeat of the drum, she was joyous.

Through the years, Elisabeth welcomed me with chocolate and had me make tea.

A kindred spirit, she freely shared her personal life, philosophy, and belief in Spirit World.

Her son, Ken, called one time and said Elisabeth wanted a traditional tipi (teepee) by her Scottsdale home. I asked my Lakota friend to make one for Elisabeth. He said he made tipis only for Sun Dancers, which my partner, Sonne, and I were. I explained the deeply humanitarian and spiritual nature of Elisabeth and he accepted. Sonne and I, Ken, and friends put up her tipi. By noon, it stood like a beautiful bride by the wooden cross nearby.

We brought Elisabeth in her wheelchair and performed an honoring ceremony for her. The pipe of soapstone and elderberry I had made for her had burned in the Shenandoah home fire with all her belongings. We smoked my sacred pipe, and it was good.

Ken called again when Elisabeth's tipi blew down in a monsoon. We were concerned with the condition of the canvas as we gently gathered it from its sandy interment. And when we finished, we were awestruck!

The tipi was covered with hundreds of eagle feathers sand-painted by the monsoon winds. I have seen many supernatural things, and this one was magnificent. I thought, when Elisabeth's body dies, her spirit will fly in the company of eagles to Spirit World. Over time, the desert winds whisked away Nature's feathered sand painting.

I watched television for Elisabeth's interview with Oprah Winfrey. It showed Oprah and her crew driving by the sun-bleached tipi, and it was good.

When Elisabeth's body began to weaken, I went more times to pray and drum to help her patiently endure her stroke. Her endurance was tested to the point that she asked for a ceremony to leave her cocooned body. I sat with Elisabeth and drummed the purification songs to prepare her spirit to fly freely when her time came. More often now, on the far saguaro, I'd see the black eagle perched like a guardian, watching and waiting for Elisabeth.

My last time with Elisabeth, I gazed into the eyes of this "Daughter of the Stars," this wise woman whose life seemed now to settle like a fading sunset at twilight. I thought, *Beloved, Brave, Elisabeth Standing Eagle, you have devoted your entire life and done so much for so many people. Do you now look to the stars and wish to fly?*

In August, when Elisabeth's spirit left her earthly body, it began its upward spiraling butterfly dance. At the funeral, my mind was seriously focused on singing her ceremonial honoring song. I called Elisabeth's spirit to come as an eagle as a sign she heard her song.

Well, most people who knew Elisabeth often heard her say, "Life is serious, so dance more, laugh more, eat more chocolate, and live!" Elisabeth was unpretentious and her sense of humor was in itself a sacred ceremony.

I began to speak to the guests, "I am Bluebird, to sing 'The Eagle Is Coming' for Elisabeth's journey to Spirit World."

On my first drumbeat, I looked for the eagle, but instead, near the lake, a gaggle of geese started honking so loud and strong that everyone broke out in pure laughter!

The Eagle has flown to the stars.

Elayne Reyna is a spiritual counselor and an elder of the San Juan Intertribal Council. A visionary and peacemaker, she is the founder of One Earth One People Peace Vision, Inc., which is dedicated to promoting peace through the arts. She has written and illustrated two books, *Wolf Dreamer* and *Song of the Bluebird*. Her visionary art is collected and sold internationally.

"To love means not to impose your
own powers on your fellow man,
but offer him your help.

If he refuses, be proud that he can
do it on his own.

To love means to live without fear
and anxieties about tomorrow.

To love means never to be afraid of
the windstorms of life.

Should you shield the canyons
from the windstorms, you would
never see the true beauty of their
carvings."

— Elisabeth Kübler-Ross, M.D.

Planetary Sisters

By Barbara Brennan, Ph.D., D.Th.

A leader in the field of energy healing, Barbara Brennan authored
the bestselling books *Hands of Light* and *Light Emerging.* It is not
unusual for people with great minds and great missions to seek each
other out. Barbara recounts one such memorable meeting.

The first time I saw Elisabeth she was on a stage in front of
several thousand people. I got as close as I could to the stage
and hunkered down on the floor in front of the people sitting in the
first row.

She held our undivided attention with loving power and presence
for several hours. Clearly, here was a woman who knew about life and
death from direct experience. Her unmatchable heart enveloped everyone in an aura of peace.

A few years later, I sent her my first book, *Hands of Light,* and asked
for an appointment to visit her. As I drove to her house, I noticed the
constellation of Pleiades was always in the sky in front of me as if the
stars were leading me to her.

When I jumped out of my car at her front porch, I asked if she knew about the Pleiades and added, "I think I'm from there."

She replied, "Yes, of course. So am I." That was the first thing we said to each other.

The evening progressed through a series of exciting conversations about healing, how the aura changes through the stages of death, various psychic experiences each had had, and even about extra-terrestrials, interrupted occasionally by some delicious goody she had baked earlier that day.

Goodies covered all the counter space in her kitchen — cakes, pies, cookies, and breads. I later heard that was normal for Elisabeth's kitchen.

I channeled for her for nine hours that evening. She asked questions on every possible subject, including the state of the world, the future, a cure for AIDS, and its origin. I left all the recordings of the channeling there. I don't know what happened to them.

The next visit was much the same as the first, except this time I left in the afternoon, and a rainbow arched over the road just in front of the car the entire way home!

After that, I saw Elisabeth occasionally at various conferences. Each time she would ask me, with great authority, if I were following guidance and doing what I was born to do. What a *great lady!*

Dr. Barbara Brennan has been researching the human energy field for more than 30 years. Her bestselling books are considered classics in the field of complementary medicine. She is founder and president of the Barbara Brennan School of Healing, and also founder of the Barbara Brennan Center for Research and Healing.

Elisabeth Was My Writing Angel

By Doreen Virtue, Ph.D.

Bestselling author Doreen Virtue became acquainted with
Elisabeth's work and was moved to push past procrastination
to pursue her own dreams.

I had just finished lecturing to a class about the influence that
Elisabeth Kübler-Ross had on my own life when someone from
my office handed me a letter inviting me to write a commentary for
the book *Tea with Elisabeth*.

This was more than synchronicity. It was the Divine influence that
had spurred Elisabeth's work, and which, in turn, had changed my life
many years ago.

I was a young mother of two sons, a part-time college student and a
secretary at an insurance firm. I was enrolled in a class called Death
and Dying, based upon Elisabeth's book by the same name, which
was our textbook. Our class field trips took us to sites associated with
death, including a crematorium, a funeral parlor, and a cemetery.

Since I was only 25 years old and had not yet lost any friends or relatives, I hadn't thought much about death. So at first I was squeamish about the topic. Then I realized that we all regularly face little deaths, such as disappointments, lost opportunities, and challenges. The stages of grief discovered by Elisabeth fit those experiences, as much as the formal death process.

I also realized that I'd been procrastinating concerning my major life dreams because I hadn't yet faced my body's mortality. I wanted to write books that helped people to heal from emotional wounds.

I'd always loved writing since I was a small girl and had wanted to be a professional writer while growing up. I'd taken many journalism courses, and had been editor of school newspapers and a hometown weekly paper.

"Someday I'll write a book," I often thought and said. During my Death and Dying class, I realized that I'd held an unconscious fantasy that someday in the future, I'd have more time to write an entire book.

I was putting off my book, waiting for that elusive day. I hadn't realized that we have only a finite number of years in which we're alive to pursue our dreams.

The class wiped away my excuses. I brought out my typewriter, put it on the kitchen table, and wrote for one hour a night after my sons went to sleep. In a few months, I had a book proposal, and a few months later, I held a publishing contract for my first book. By the time I was 30 years old, I had two books published. I'm now 46 and have had nearly 30 books published.

If it weren't for Elisabeth's book, which helped me to face my mortality, I might have waited forever to write. Thanks to Elisabeth, I realized that now is the time to take action upon our dreams. Although our souls are immortal, our bodies won't last forever. We need to use our precious time on earth making contributions with our natural talents and interests.

Thank you, Elisabeth! You are my writing angel.

Dr. Doreen Virtue is a retired counseling psychologist. In 1995 she was "saved by an angel" during an armed car-jacking in Anaheim, California. This experience was the impetus for a life devoted to researching, writing, and speaking about angels. Her most recent book is *The Miracles of Archangel Michael*. She is a featured guest on national network television shows, including *Oprah* and *Good Morning America*.

My Sister's Comfort

By Marianne Williamson

Bestselling author Marianne Williamson was touched by Elisabeth's
work through the death of her sister, Jane.

The first time I ever heard of Elisabeth Kübler-Ross was from
my sister in the 1970s. Jane was a third-grade teacher, and her
work had no obvious connection to Elisabeth's. However, she was
fascinated by Kübler-Ross's work with death and dying and often
showed me her books with great enthusiasm.

About 10 years later, Jane was diagnosed with breast cancer. During the five years of her struggle, before she died in 1994, she often
pointed out the irony of her longtime interest in Elisabeth Kübler-
Ross.

The doctors had told Jane that the cancer had probably been in her
system for a decade or so before it became symptomatic. I think, and
I believe Jane did too, that subconsciously she *knew* about her cancer
from its inception, thus her interest in the work of Kübler-Ross. She

181

was seeking to prepare for her death before she even consciously knew that she would die.

I saw Kübler-Ross on television once, and she was speaking of a vision she had experienced. A woman she had worked with who, having already died, visited Elisabeth at her office to urge her to continue with her work no matter what. Kübler-Ross demanded that the woman sign her name on a piece of paper to "prove" her existence. She did.

Kübler-Ross believed it was a real visitation, and so do I. And I know my sister would have made the same visit if she had the opportunity to do so. Jane knew firsthand the profound comfort of Elisabeth's teaching and would have wished it for everyone who needed it.

Kübler-Ross and I shared the same birthday. We also shared a mutual close friend. While I never met her personally, she was an inspiration to me and will remain so. She was a woman who spoke her truth, however much others sought to marginalize it; who remained true to her convictions, however much others sought to belittle them; and helped thousands, perhaps millions, of others because of what she did.

As a woman and as a visionary, Kübler-Ross set an example that means a lot to me. Most important of all, she gave great comfort to someone I loved.

Now that she too has passed on…may she rest in joy.

Marianne Williamson is an internationally acclaimed bestselling author, lecturer, and spiritual teacher. Four of her books have been number one on the New York Times bestsellers list: *A Return to Love, Iluminata, Everyday Grace*, and *A Woman's Worth*. She cofounded The Peace Alliance, a worldwide network of peace activists who are working together to use nonviolence as a positive social force.

*"We must all learn to love,
and to love unconditionally."*

— Elisabeth Kübler-Ross, M.D.

My Experience with Elisabeth Kübler-Ross

(Translated from Spanish)

By Juan Francisco "Frank" Aráuz

Frank Aráuz is a physician from Nicaragua who speaks the language
of the heart perfectly. He became one of Elisabeth's most trusted
and loved caregivers during her last years of life.

E lisabeth Kübler-Ross was one of the most admirable and extraordinary individuals I ever met. Through her acute human sensitivity, her teachings, and her writings, she was a symbol to me of a person who lived, worked, and fought for a world with less pain, more love, and more justice.

Like everyone else who knew her, I have a story to tell. I also realize while writing this that I still hold so much emotion concerning her death.

I seized the opportunity to participate in this book to celebrate Elisabeth Kübler-Ross. I want to share some of the experiences I had with her during her stay at Leisure Living, the assisted-living home where I work and where she lived for the last two years of her life.

On a warm afternoon in October 2002, Elisabeth arrived at this house, accompanied by one of her nieces, Susan, and Kenneth Ross, her son. After smoking a cigarette and drinking a cup of coffee, a little shy but very determined, she moved into the room that was prepared for her, where she would live the last chapter of her sacrificial, fruitful life.

Little by little and as the days went by, I got to know her health, her needs, her preferences, and her personality. Likewise, I began relating to her family and to the many friends who visited her from many parts of the U.S. and the world. With this knowledge as a basis, I organized a work routine that could guarantee her a certain grade of comfort and tranquility in the midst of her delicate health.

In Elisabeth Kübler-Ross I met an intelligent person quick in her mind and actions. She was a true friend with a spontaneous disposition that automatically moved her to help ease the pain and the difficult situation of those who suffered or had a problem. This was also a woman with a deep maternal instinct, as from her bed she always cared about the health and well-being of her children and grandchildren.

With the purpose of entertaining her and keeping her motivated, I told her about my life, my family, and my goals.

She assisted me with improving my English, as well as my disposition concerning my job, and I learned to see the future with more optimism. To Elisabeth I was more than a caretaker — I was also a trusted friend. Frequently, Elisabeth exalted my name before her visitors, telling them that I was the best "doctor," the best chef in the world, and number one in everything. Those comments were so satisfying because I knew that I was fulfilling my programmed goals of helping her enjoy her last days.

Her personality fluctuated with her moods. Sometimes she was very angry concerning her situation. But she also had moments of great humor. She loved to joke, play, and laugh hard. That filled me with satisfaction, knowing her joy and happiness were contagious.

Because of her health the last year, her lucid periods alternated with confusion. For some time she would mentally organize a tour to different countries, to which I was invited. She would begin with Austria, where she would found a hospice, then we would go to Switzerland to visit her family, and later we would meet some friends in Japan and Australia. On our way home, we would visit my family in Nicaragua. This tour was never taken, of course, yet I hope I am able to do it someday in her honor.

One way or another, without it being my goal, she became quite dependent on me. She even rejected the attentions and the caring of the personnel of hospice and of my co-workers.

As the days went by, her health deteriorated further and with that her quality of life. Moments of frustration, anger, depression, and pain began alternating, without reaching the desired result of transition.

I tried in every way possible to prolong her life, although she did not cooperate much. For example, I prepared her favorite finger food and snacks so she would eat, but still she didn't want to. I began using her family to get her to eat. I'd say, "This is for Emma," and she ate, "and this is for Sylvia, for Barbara, for Kenneth." After this, she'd tell me she didn't want any more. Then I would tell her, "This is for Frank." At that, she kind of reacted, opened her eyes, smiled, and then she'd say, "Give me two."

Many times when I prepared something, to make sure she'd eat, I asked her if it was good. And she'd say no. I began to worry, and when I asked her what was wrong, she would tell me, "It is not good because it is excellent."

Elisabeth's life was reaching its end, and with that, the culmination of her long journey. For me, it was hard to accept the reality. Even though I had experienced the death of patients from irreversible causes throughout my medical career in Nicaragua, this was different. I had come to care deeply for Elisabeth during our time together. On August 24, 2004, Elisabeth Kübler-Ross died at 10:00 a.m., leaving an emptiness and sadness in the hearts of all those who loved and cherished her, but at the same time, relief and resignation as well because her pain and suffering had finally ended. Meeting and caring for Elisabeth Kübler-Ross was an enlightening experience and at the same time, an honor and a privilege, because I was allowed to give back to her some of the many kindnesses she gave to thousands of needy people for so many years.

Juan Francisco "Frank" Aráuz came to the U.S. from Nicaragua in 2001. He received his medical degree in 1990 from a University in Lugansk, Ukraine. Because of stringent U.S. requirements, he is not yet permitted to practice medicine in America.

The Touch of Love

By Elizabeth F. "Bette" Croce, B.S.N., R.N.

For more than 40 years, this consummate caregiver has devoted
her life to easing the pain of dying for individuals and their families.
When Elisabeth crossed her path in 1996, she was automatically
included in the circle of love.

Since the beginning of my nursing career, my heart has been drawn
to the bedside of the dying, to help them live out their lives in
comfort. My initial hospice training was with an organization called
Heartbeat, and although I was unaware of it at the time, it began in the
same era and in the same part of the country where Elisabeth Kübler-
Ross was pioneering her work with the dying.

The motto of the Heartbeat organization is: "The heart of a woman
is not her own, it beats for everyone she has known." Elisabeth Kübler-
Ross, who has always been one of the greatest influences in my life and
work, has lived this motto more than anyone I have known. I never
dreamed I would have the opportunity to meet her in person.

While in the hospital visiting one of my hospice patients, I saw her. She was in a wheelchair recovering from a fractured hip. The next day she was in my patient's room comforting him and his wife. Before I knew it, I was helping Elisabeth into bed. After my patient died, and Elisabeth was back in her home, she would ask me to dial the wife's number so she could invite her to come for a visit. It was a humbling experience to witness Elisabeth's total commitment to giving, from her heart, in such an intense, comforting, healing manner.

As I continued to visit her, I would often discuss a difficult situation a patient or family member was having. She would be very interested, and quickly have just the perfect answer I needed to help. I remember clearly her instruction that "You never break someone's denial." This was the beginning of an adventure with Elisabeth that spanned nine years, and included hundreds of visits and many cups of tea.

Because of her immobility, she always wanted two cups of tea left within her reach. Everything she thought she would need was stacked around her and seemingly defied the laws of gravity. When she would say, "Put the tea on the top of the stacks," I learned the power of positive thinking. If I even thought they would fall, she would know it, and would sternly, but laughingly, admonish me. I pride myself on the fact that I never spilled a cup of tea.

I vividly remember the day we talked about her going on hospice service. Expressing much joy as she signed the hospice admission forms, she happily stated, "I'm finally a hospice patient," thinking that her suffering would soon be over. This was not to be for several more years, during which time she struggled to adjust from dying to living.

Being so fiercely independent didn't prepare her for having to rely on others for her basic needs, which was not her "cup of tea." Her angry side was often directed at those who loved and cared for her, teaching us compassion and acceptance. I promised myself that I would be available to make her life as comfortable and happy as possible. I would call her, whenever the spirit moved me, and I would hear her voice on the end of the line saying, "I need you," and I would be on my way.

We'd watch TV together, often with teary eyes. When she wanted to know when a favorite show such as *The X Files* or *Little House on the Prairie* was on, she'd be annoyed when I couldn't figure it out quick enough, and say, "Call your daughters to get the time and channel."

Elisabeth loved getting presents, and giving them as well. One day I noticed she had a new E.T. with hands held upward. I commented that E.T. was doing TT (Therapeutic Touch, energy healing which she knew I practiced). The next time I saw her — surprise! She had a big box wrapped up for me with E.T. inside. Now it has a special place in my home.

When she was up to it, Elisabeth loved to shop — I'd say to the extreme. She especially loved the big health food markets. They always seemed to have narrow and crowded aisles, which made maneuvering Elisabeth in her wheelchair a great challenge. Because she was so sensitive to pain when touched, she would threaten a "karate chop" to anyone who bumped into her, sometimes me.

As her life drew to a close, I remembered that years ago I had coordinated the Completing the Circle of Life for the Nurse-Healers Professional Associates International Conference, a conference on dying. A ceremony honoring Elisabeth was included. She was unable to attend but was very pleased and wanted to be kept informed about the plans and activities.

Participants in the conference wrote love notes to her and brought rocks to be blessed during a Native American Cornmeal Ceremony. Instructions were provided describing how to create a Butterfly Garden in Elisabeth's honor at hospices, health facilities, or homes. A beautiful Butterfly Garden was dedicated at the Casey House AIDS Hospice in Toronto, Canada. Many others are still being developed worldwide.

My last visit to Elisabeth was brief as she was ready to graduate. Her son, daughter, and granddaughters were with her. I sensed her warm heart, and I began whispering repeatedly, "Thank you, I love you," not only for myself, but for everyone she has touched.

Elisabeth loved to receive flowers, and I had told her I would continue to bring them to her burial site. On a recent visit, the grass was covered with hundreds of ducks and geese munching on the plants and ornaments. As several groups took off in perfect formations, I felt Elisabeth's delightful presence among them. I took it as sign that she had "made it!" Thank you, Elisabeth. Enjoy the flight.

Bette Croce's extensive nursing career includes more than 25 years of ongoing hospice work. She is a Therapeutic Touch teacher and practitioner, and for over a decade has practiced, studied, and taught Chinese medical Qigong. She is currently pursuing a master's degree in holistic health counseling.

Anything Is Possible

By Rose Winters

A friend who loved and helped Elisabeth through the last years of
her life, learns a lesson in possibilities.

Elisabeth was my friend for nearly 15 years. She was a woman
who loved to laugh, worked hard, demanded much, and expected more. She was always bigger than life. Yet what I remember
most about Elisabeth are the ordinary interactions I had with her.

In Elisabeth's home, next to her sturdy hospital bed, she had a simple
wooden TV tray, just your usual 20-inch by 15-inch variety. To look at
such a small stand, you wouldn't think it could hold very much. But she
kept the most vital elements of her life there on that tray. Nothing could
be moved without her notice or her raised voice. It's how she taught me
geometry.

Whenever I was with her before she went to bed, she wanted tea
and her unfinished dinner placed on that small, *very* small, TV tray.
She wanted two cups of English Breakfast Black Tea and two cups of

Mandarin Orange, hot, each with straws for easy sipping and each with two teaspoons of sugar.

Why would such a simple act require geometry? What you need to know is what else was on this small table before the cups of tea could be added. It held: multiple medication bottles, two packages of opened Dunhill cigarettes, an ashtray, a few cigarette lighters, a flashlight, bars of real Swiss Chocolate — not American or any other plastic-tasting, poor imitation of the real chocolate that only the Swiss can make (as she was very quick to point out) — a baggie with two or three slices of salami, several miniature rounds of Laughing Cow Mini Babybel original, semi-soft cheese with the rind slightly pulled for easy opening, and another baggie with several slices of French baguette, buttered.

All of this in case she got hungry during the night. Then there was the telephone, a piece of paper that was sacred — with do-not-touch signs with "danger of damnation" invisibly written all over it along with the names and numbers of family and friends — a pen, a recent letter or two, and a few dollars tucked under the telephone. It was on this *very* crowded space that she expected four cups of tea to be added without removing anything. Elisabeth spoke several languages fluently, yet she never learned how to accept "It can't be done" in any of them.

I never knew what she was going to ask me to do. One December morning several years ago, Elisabeth excitedly showed me a Christmas card she had just received from Sarah Ferguson, the Duchess of York. She was tickled that it included a picture of the Duchess with her lovely family. She wanted to immediately send her a note and a Christmas card.

She said, "You must call the palace and get her address so I can send her a card." I asked, "You want *me* to call the palace?" She gave me that look she got when someone dared be stupid in her presence and answered, "Naturally. Here is the number. Call."

I spend most of my working days on the telephone so it is not a foreign experience to me. Yet, somehow, calling the palace seemed completely different. I had butterflies in my stomach and quaking in my knees as I began dialing. In my head, I was repeating my mantra for such occasions: "Don't screw up. Don't screw up."

As the telephone began to ring, Elisabeth reached out and kicked me with her good foot to get my attention and said, "Don't call her Fergie. She is the Duchess of York." Now with my quaking knees, butterflies dancing in my stomach, I added to my mantra of "Don't screw up," "Don't say Fergie."

With all of this swirling in my head, and with Elisabeth within easy kicking distance, I heard, "This is Shirley." I thought, *Don't screw up. Don't say, Fergie. Shirley? What a friendly name for a palace receptionist.*

I said, "This is Rose Winters calling on behalf of Dr. Elisabeth Kübler-Ross. (Foot came out. Elisabeth mouthed: "Don't say Fergie.") I swallowed and continued. "Dr. Ross would like to send a Christmas card to Sarah, the Duchess of York. May we have her mailing address, please?" I breathed out.

Shirley said, "What?" I thought, *Wow. The palace is much more casual than I thought.* Concentrating as hard as I could, I repeated who I was and why I was calling, being very careful not to say, "Fergie." Elisabeth looked at me skeptically, like somehow I was messing up.

Shirley asked again, "Who are you calling?" I wondered if perhaps I had dialed the wrong palace. I nervously repeated my message. I thought I was being very clear and was actually quite proud of myself for not screwing up.

Shirley, however, immediately went into hysterics and said to those apparently around her: "She's calling the palace! She wants to reach the Duchess!"

By this time I was standing there in great confusion, wondering how one reports unprofessional telephone behavior to the palace. Finally, Shirley sputtered, "You have the wrong number. This is Motorola!"

I meekly hung up the phone and looked at Elisabeth. She demanded an explanation. I told her. She shook her head, crossed herself, then both of us laughed so hard the tears came.

Elisabeth often asked of me, demanded even, the impossible. It wasn't that she believed in me so much as it was that she believed in possibilities. Whatever her intention, her perspective expanded to accommodate its successful completion — whether it meant calling the palace, adding four cups of tea to a crowded table, or moving the world to more compassionate care of the dying. It was from the everyday experiences with her that I learned if you let go of preconceived ideas and act as if something is possible, it is.

Rose Winters is executive director of For the Children Foundation, a non-profit organization she established to create an intentional world for children. She has extensive experience in the non-profit field, and continues as a consultant to governmental and non-profit agencies addressing the concerns of children and youth. She is also co-founder and co-publisher of *One Planet* magazine.

Like a Good Neighbor…

By Hope Sacharoff

Those who knew Elisabeth's challenges during the last years of her life can only imagine what it would have been like to be her on-call neighbor. Her handmaiden Hope more than met the challenge.

By March of 1998, I had been part of Elisabeth's company of handmaidens for over two years. Since Elisabeth and I were neighbors and friends, I was on her list as her number one helper.

My initial voluntary role was to assist her with the incredible amount of mail she received each day, but this soon expanded. As our relationship grew into friendship, and as her health deteriorated, she would become like family. I knew her when she was angry and struggling with her own issues; after all, she was human, too.

Having so much of her life taken away from her by being partially incapacitated caused her to react in a way that was natural and appropriate for her. She, too, was working her way through her own life issues. It has been said many times by many people that Elisabeth was not a phony baloney. What you saw was what you got.

Whatever we learned as her handmaidens during that time would not be easy. Nothing worthwhile ever is, but how blessed I was along with so many others to have "hung in there." Yes, there were those moments that I could do no wrong. And then, there were other moments. I have so many memories of my time with Elisabeth, but I would like to share the two that were of greatest significance to me.

It wasn't long before my husband, Howard, and I were both on call. There were times I couldn't do what Elisabeth needed me to do because I am vertically challenged (at only four feet, 11 inches). Lifting or doing anything requiring strength were simply things I could not do. So Howard became a very necessary part of our relationship, and he and Elisabeth had a delightful rapport. She always seemed to brighten at his presence.

Toward the end of March, Elisabeth's sister Eva was coming to visit, and we all were looking forward to her arrival. I invited Elisabeth and her sister to come to lunch at our house, which was nearby. Surprisingly she agreed, making us both very happy.

The time arrived and so did our honored guests. We enjoyed our lunch together very much. Following lunch, Elisabeth asked to be taken out on to the patio where both Howard and Eva joined her. Elisabeth, lighting up her cigarette, looked so at ease and comfortable in her new surroundings. As I looked out the window right above the sink where I was doing the dishes, I saw the three of them chatting animatedly about life in New York, and in the Bronx specifically. I never realized that they both had spent time in the neighborhood where Howard and I had so many memories.

I got the sense that this was family catching up on old times. There was a very warm feeling about that wonderful encounter. It seemed as if for a short time that Elisabeth forgot the bitterness, the wheel-chair, and the challenges, as she relished being in the glow of family and friends.

It also made me realize how difficult life had become for this dynamic woman so used to going anywhere in the world on a moment's notice in the service of others. It seemed some part of the cosmic puzzle, that the one who repeatedly reminded us all that we are here to serve unconditionally now needed that very gift.

The second significant encounter occurred much later. It was in August of 2004. Howard and I had made plans to go to Lake Tahoe to celebrate my birthday near the end of the month. At the time Elisabeth's condition was already quite fragile.

I asked Howard if he would please drop me off at the assisted-care home so that I might sing for Elisabeth. She loved music, and when she realized I could sing, she had shared with me her favorite songs.

Knocking gently at the door, I inquired if it was too early to visit. They assured me it was fine. I entered her room quietly. She seemed to be sleeping. There was a chair beside the bed. I sat down and began singing my special folder of Elisabeth music, including "Edelweiss," "The Rose," "Perhaps Love," and the "Sabbath Prayer" from *Fiddler on the Roof*.

After I sang the "Sabbath Prayer," I looked over and noticed the great ease with which she was resting. She opened her eyes and said, "I liked it. I liked it."

For me there would never be any higher praise or louder applause that warmed my heart or soul more than those six words. On that particular day I sang for two-and-a-half hours.

While we were in Lake Tahoe, early on the morning of August 25, Howard awakened at 4:30 a.m. for no apparent reason. He was moved to turn on the hotel television, and in doing so, noticed a few remaining words left on the crawl at the bottom of the screen, which mentioned "noted psychiatrist" and also her place in history with hospice. He called out telling me that it was over, that she was gone.

As we began touring the area that day, we noticed the abundance of place-names that were reminiscent of Switzerland. Her presence was palpable. Later that day, as we sat having lunch overlooking the sun-emblazoned lake, we lifted our glasses of iced tea and honored her. We needed to express our gratitude for having known her, for her allowing us to love her, and for our best wishes for her safe trip Home.

Hope Sacharoff is an actress. She has performed on stage in New York and Illinois, including playing the role of Yenta in *Fiddler on the Roof*. Her last movie before relocating to Arizona was Woody Allen's *Bullets Over Broadway*. She has also appeared in numerous commercials for national corporations.

Tea with Elisabeth

By Fern Stewart Welch

Another handmaiden is drawn to love and serve Elisabeth, and
discovers the gift that keeps on giving.

I first met Elisabeth after she moved to Scottsdale, Arizona, in
1994. She was a good friend of Gladys T. McGarey, M.D.,
M.D.(H), and at that time I was executive director of the holistic
medical foundation that bore Dr. Gladys' name. We took tea with
Elisabeth at her house in Scottsdale, and thus I began my relationship
with her.

Elisabeth agreed to come onto the advisory board of the foundation, and my interaction with her increased. Out of respect for her
privacy, however, I maintained a strictly professional relationship with
her. When it was time for me to leave the foundation in 1999, due to
my husband's failing health, I gave her a courtesy farewell call.

She listened to me and said, "When are you coming out to see me?"
I sputtered for a few moments trying to explain that I had no official

reason to come and see her. She insisted, "Fern, what does that have to do with anything? When are you coming out to see me?" She called me each week thereafter until I began visiting her, and this marked the beginning of our friendship.

The hallmark of the time I spent with Elisabeth through the following years was a bond that seemed to be there from the beginning, and now was allowed to flourish. She seemed to enjoy my company, as I did hers. She trusted me, and I was humbled and protective of this.

I soon learned which delectable desserts from a local gourmet grocery were her favorites, and these graced our teatimes. Taking tea with Elisabeth was synonymous with a visit with her. You were hardly inside the door before she asked someone to put the kettle on for tea.

When several friends and I picked her up one day and took her out to the desert for afternoon tea, she seemed surprisingly quiet as we set up a table amid the glorious spring flowers. She later told me this was the only time in her life she had ever been alone with women in such an informal situation.

I discovered that she loved cream of asparagus soup, and this became one of my specialties. I treasure the times when she hungrily devoured the soup, and the homemade cornbread slathered with sweet butter, which she told me was the best ever. I also hold to my heart that as her health failed, she would allow me to feed her and offer tender endearments, such as I had used with my own children and grandchildren.

We also shared a love of dancing, and one of the joys of my life was attending a party for her at which she "danced" with at least eight of her longtime male friends. Each man lifted her lovingly out of the wheelchair — placed her tiny feet on his — and grandly swirled her around the room to her favorite music. Her obvious delight was matched only by the joy of those who loved her and shared in the moment.

She loved to laugh, and laughter came very easy. Nothing pleased her more than for a lighthearted repartee to continue until we dissolved in laughter. One time I was holding a glass of ice-cold lemonade for her at her bedside when she inadvertently hit the glass with her arm, and some of the icy contents splashed onto her chest.

She was very sensitive to cold and was really startled. I felt terrible, and the more I apologized, the more she laughed. While I was trying to clean up the spill and keep her warm, my efforts and pleas to God for forgiveness brought forth even more laughter. When she finally said, "He's enjoying it, too," I was able to give in to laughter also, and the rest of the visit was embraced in the warm glow of shared frivolity.

When the Swiss Embassy held a premiere of the documentary of her life at a theater in Scottsdale, I arranged to get her favorite red silk Chinese-style dress out of storage, bought her new shoes, and drove to pick her up. She was bright-eyed, her skin flushed, and she had been ready to go hours before I arrived. As wearied as she was by the outing, on the drive home she was still able to give me a cogent and thorough analysis of the film's merits.

I remember the look on her face when I came in one day with a beautiful bouquet of red roses for her, and finding out this just happened to be the anniversary of her beloved husband's death. Her energy rose immediately, and she announced that she felt his presence as I entered the room. Then she happily recounted a memory of Manny that involved red roses.

When my husband, Kenneth, was nearing the death process, Elisabeth was there for me. She also asked to read the manuscript I was writing to chronicle his lengthy decline and death. At that time it had the working title, *One Ordinary Person's Journey to God*. After reading it, she awarded me her highest commendation: "This is not phony baloney. It is your love affair with you, your husband, and God."

After Ken's death she telephoned me to tell me again that she loved what I had written, and that I must finish it. After hanging up I was so moved that I burst into tears. The phone rang again immediately. It was Elisabeth with a terse comment: "And change the title," she said. "You are not an ordinary person!"

I immediately went to the computer, and for the first time in several months began working on the manuscript. Once again I dissolved into tears and sobbing. Each day as I worked on in spite of the tears, I realized I was drawn to the book with a passion and commitment I had never known before. As I completed the last chapters of the book, the title presented itself, *The Heart Knows the Way — How to Follow Your Heart to a Conscious Connection with the Divine Spirit Within.*

I believe Elisabeth provided the inspiration I needed to continue with the healing process, my life, and the book. She loved the new title and blessed it with a wonderful endorsement.

Each time I shared with her that I was becoming stronger due to the experience with my husband, she said with mixed pride and impatience, "It's about time!"

Even though she was chronologically my senior, my dreams of her seemed to confirm the protective, motherly feelings I had toward her. I believe she was my baby in another lifetime.

In one of my last dreams about Elisabeth, she was standing behind me holding my arms upright, supporting me when weariness overtook me. Now I know that it was her evolutionary work in changing the way the world thinks about death and dying that empowered me to seek a better, more loving, and enlightened way to assist my husband in his final life journey — and then to write and speak about the experience. I can hear Elisabeth's laughter as she once again says, "It's about time!"

Fern Stewart Welch is a veteran writer and author of two books, *You Can Live A Balanced Life In An Unbalanced World,* and *The Heart Knows the Way — How to Follow Your Heart to a Conscious Connection with the Divine Spirit Within.* The tribute she wrote for Elisabeth's memorial service was the inspiration for *Tea with Elisabeth.*

"Know your own self,
and view life as a challenge,
where the hardest choices are
the highest ones, the ones that
resonate with righteousness,
and provide the strength and
insight of Him, the Highest of
the High."

— Elisabeth Kübler-Ross, M.D.

A Profile of Elisabeth Kübler-Ross, M.D.

July 8, 1926 – August 24, 2004

In 1926 triplets were born to an obscure, Swiss couple named Kübler, an event rare enough at that time to be treated as major news. The firstborn, a girl the parents named Elisabeth, became the focus of attention because at two pounds she was so small and fragile.

What no one could have foreseen was that this tiny human being would become a world-renowned physician, psychiatrist, thanatologist, author, pioneer, and an international icon.

Her greatest influence came from her writings. In 1969 she identified the five stages of dying in her seminal book, *On Death and Dying,* which resulted from interviewing thousands of terminally ill patients.

It was this revolutionary book, and Elisabeth's incredible courage and spirit that literally transformed how the world views death and dying, and brought compassion and dignity to the dying process.

But the worldwide successes of Elisabeth Kübler-Ross were not without great personal sacrifice and pain. They would cost her a teaching position at the University of Chicago Medical School, her marriage to neuropathologist Dr. Emanuel R. Ross, and the daily care of their children, Kenneth and Barbara.

Following *On Death and Dying,* she wrote more than 20 books. Her works have been printed in 27 languages, read by millions, and used in colleges and universities and as required textbooks in medical schools around the world.

She was the leading force behind mainstreaming the hospice movement in the United States. She became a popular international lecturer and facilitated her Life, Death, and Transition workshops around the world.

Throughout her life, Elisabeth Kübler-Ross jumped in where even angels feared to tread. She never shied away from controversy or challenges so it isn't a surprise that she turned her focus to helping those with HIV/AIDS early in the epidemic.

Elisabeth officially retired to Arizona in 1995 after a series of debilitating strokes affected her body, and after a fire destroyed her home in Headwaters, Virginia.

Despite her personal travails, Elisabeth spent her life bringing comfort and understanding to millions facing death or the deaths of their loved ones. Even after her health began to decline and she was confined to a wheelchair, she continued ministering to the hundreds of people who came seeking her compassionate wisdom.

For her pioneering contributions, she received innumerable honors and awards from organizations worldwide, including being the recipient of more than 20 honorary degrees. In 1999 *Time* magazine named her one of the "Greatest Minds" of this century.

She died on August 24, 2004, mourned by millions of people whose lives had been made better by her indomitable spirit, energy, and compassion. In 2007, she was inducted posthumously into the National Women's Hall of Fame.

For more information visit: www.elisabethkublerross.com

Photo Gallery

Elisabeth as a medical school student in Switzerland

Elisabeth and Manny in Switzerland

Elisabeth and Manny on their wedding day

Elisabeth in Luxor, Egypt, where she was invited to lecture by the Saddat family

Elisabeth and son Ken in Sydney, Australia

Elisabeth and Manny in Salt Lake City, Utah, at daughter Barbara's graduation

Elisabeth with daughter Barbara in Salt Lake City, Utah, in the early 1990s

Elisabeth with her nieces,
Susan Elisabeth Bacher (left) and Vreni Aeberli.

Elisabeth's grandchildren Emma and
Sylvia Rothweiler

Elisabeth and sister Eva Kübler-Bacher in
Scottsdale, Arizona, in 1994

Mal Warshaw, photographer, collaborated with Elisabeth on the books *To Live Until We Say Goodbye* and *Working It Through*. Warshaw took hundreds of candid photos of Elisabeth during her working years. Below, his pictures capture Elisabeth visiting with dying adults and children, connecting with participants attending her workshops, and facilitating support group meetings.

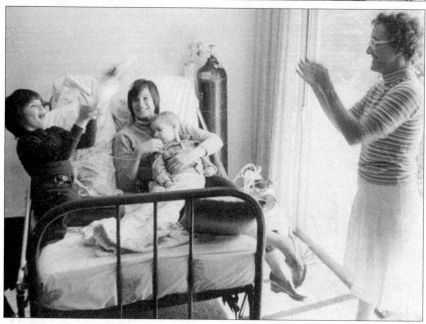

The Elisabeth Kübler-Ross Foundation

A portion of the proceeds from the sale of *Tea with Elisabeth* will be donated to the Elisabeth Kübler-Ross Foundation (EKRF).

The mission of the non-profit foundation is to continue to support dying patients and grieving families on a comprehensive, community level, based on Dr. Kübler-Ross's principles surrounding death and dying.

The Elisabeth Kübler-Ross Foundation plans to build a Community Compassion Center — The Elisabeth House — in Phoenix, Arizona, which will be an all-inclusive grief intervention-education facility. It will provide the community with support groups, individual counseling, workshops, art and music therapy, library and media resources, as well as continuing education for health-care professionals. EKRF will partner in this project with the MISS Foundation, an international non-profit group that provides aid, support, and advocacy to grieving families experiencing the death of an infant or child.

For more information visit: www.ekrfoundation.org.

In Memoriam

Gregg M. Furth, Ph.D.: We knew that Dr. Furth, a dear, longtime friend of Elisabeth's, might not live to see the publishing of this book. He was a kindred spirit whose shared memories and love for Elisabeth was indicative of the wonderful camaraderie that embraced the *Tea with Elisabeth* project.

Dame Cicely Saunders, M.D.: We were deeply saddened by the death of this venerable and much honored woman who was a pioneer in the field of palliative medicine and founder of the international hospice movement.

Florence Wald, M.N., M.S., F.A.A.N.: One of the acknowledged leaders of the hospice movement, along with Drs. Kübler-Ross and Dame Cicely Saunders, she will be greatly missed for her pioneering work in promoting and providing humane care for end-of-life patients.

We salute these wonderful souls, their lives, and their work on behalf of humanity.

Contributor Profiles

Muhammad Ali

Muhammad Ali is considered by many to be the best boxer of all time. Dubbed the "Athlete of the Century" by *USA Today* and *GQ* magazine and "Sportsman of the Century" by *Sports Illustrated,* he continues to receive accolades for his contributions to sports.

After retiring from boxing, he worked tirelessly for countless charities, raising millions of dollars for their programs. For his humanitarian efforts, Muhammad has received numerous awards. In addition to being honored by Amnesty International with its Lifetime Achievement Award, the former Secretary General of the United Nations bestowed upon him the citation of United Nations Messenger of Peace. In 2005, he received the United States of America's highest civilian award, the Presidential Medal of Freedom.

Whether promoting tolerance and understanding, feeding the hungry, studying his religion, or reaching out to children in need, Muhammad Ali is devoted to making the world a better place for all people. Many believe that no other athlete has ever contributed more to the life of his country, or the world, than Muhammad Ali.

Juan Francisco "Frank" Aráuz

Juan Francisco "Frank" Aráuz came to the U.S. from Nicaragua in 2001. He received his medical degree in 1990 from a University in Lugansk, Ukraine. Because of stringent U.S. requirements, he is not yet permitted to practice medicine in America. He was Elisabeth's favorite caregiver in an assisted-living facility where she spent the last years of her life.

Eva Kübler-Bacher

Eva Bacher is a sister of Dr. Elisabeth Kübler-Ross and the only surviving triplet. She emigrated to New York in 1958 and worked for a time at the New York Swiss Tourist Office before returning to Zurich, Switzerland. She and her husband, Peter, have two daughters, Verena Eva and Susan Elisabeth.

Susan Elisabeth Bacher

Susan Bacher, Dr. Kübler-Ross's niece, is a craniosacral therapist who also teaches dance, yoga, and gymnastics. She resides in Basel, Switzerland, and travels often to India to study yoga, and to Hawaii to swim with the dolphins.

Barbara Brennan, Ph.D., D.Th.

Dr. Barbara Brennan has been researching the Human Energy Field for more than 30 years. Her bestselling books *Hands of Light*® and *Light Emerging* are considered classics in the field of complementary medicine.

Her work has resulted in the development of Brennan Healing Science®, a holistic healing modality based on the human energy-consciousness system and its relationship to health and disease. The work combines high-sense perception skills and hands-on energy healing techniques to assist individuals with their personal process of healing.

She is the founder and president of the Barbara Brennan School of Healing® in the United States, and Barbara Brennan International, Inc., which operates the Barbara Brennan School of Healing Europe®. She is also the founder of the Barbara Brennan Center for Research and Healing, a non-profit, research organization.

Joanne Cacciatore, Ph.D., LMSW

Dr. Cacciatore, founder and CEO of the MISS Foundation, is an expert in traumatic loss and child death in families. She is also a researcher and professor at Arizona State University where she spearheaded the first graduate Certificate in Trauma and Bereavement program in the nation. Her research has been published in peer-reviewed journals such as *Death Studies,* the *Omega Journal of Death and Dying,* and *Families in Society.* Her work has also been featured in *People Magazine,* the *New York Times,* the *Boston Globe,* the *Los Angeles Times,* and on CNN and National Public Radio. She received the prestigious Hon Kachina Award in 2007, and has been listed since 2006 in *Who's Who* and *Who's Who of American Women.*

She received her Doctorate from the University of Nebraska-Lincoln, and her undergraduate and Masters degrees in psychology from Arizona State University.

Diane Cirincione, Ph.D.

Dr. Diane Cirincione is a therapist and former post-doctoral clinical researcher at Langley Porter Psychiatric Institute at the University of California, San Francisco. She is an internationally known lecturer and author, as well as an entrepreneur with 30 years business experience, including owning four companies.

Dr. Cirincione is co-founder with Barbara Marx Hubbard of *The Regenopause Dialogues,* which revalue and redefine the stages of women's lives. She serves as vice-president of the Jampolsky Outreach Foundation, a non-profit group responding to worldwide requests to introduce and mentor culturally appropriate adaptations of Attitudinal Healing.

She is the author of *Sounds of the Morning Sun* and *The Identification of Relationships Between Women Witnessing Spousal Abuse in Childhood and Psychological Symptomatic Distress in Adulthood*. She also co-authored six books with her husband, Dr. Gerald Jampolsky.

D. Brookes Cowan, Ph.D., M.S.W.

Dr. D. Brookes Cowan is a medical sociologist and gerontologist and end-of-life specialist. She has taught in the Sociology Department at the University of Vermont since 1983. She served as the founding chair of the Madison-Deane Initiative, a non-profit organization focused on educating professional and lay communities about quality end-of-life care; she was involved in the making of the documentary *Pioneers of Hospice: Changing the Face of Dying*. The critically acclaimed documentary earned the National Hospice and Palliative Care Organization's 2004 award for Best Documentary for Professional Audiences. As a grief therapist and hospice volunteer since 1978, Dr. Cowan had the privilege of being called to Arizona to coordinate the care of Elisabeth Kübler-Ross during the last week of her life. Dr. Cowan also participated in the Robert Wood Johnson's Promoting Excellence in End-of-Life Care workgroup on Huntington's Disease.

Elizabeth F. "Bette" Croce, B.S.N., R.N.

Bette Croce's extensive nursing career includes more than 25 years of hospice experience. She is a teacher and practitioner of Therapeutic Touch, and for more than 18 years has practiced, studied, and taught Chinese medical Qigong. She is the Arizona Networker for Nurse Healers Professional Associates International, and serves on the education committee. She is currently studying for a Master's degree in holistic health counseling.

Ryoko Dozono, M.D.

D r. Ryoko Dozono was born in Tokyo, and graduated from Keio University School of Medicine in 1971. From 1977 to 1980, she was a research fellow at the University of Southern California School of Medicine. In 1984, she started the International Medicine Crossing Office, which combined Oriental and Western medicine. In 2001, she established the Japan Charter of the Elisabeth Kübler-Ross Center, which is headquartered in her medical office. In 2007, she published the Japanese edition of *Tea with Elisabeth*.

Anneloes Eterman

A nneloes Eterman is a nurse and an art/drama therapist who specializes in working with spontaneous drawings and care for the caregivers. After the birth of her baby, Femke, who was born with an open spine and died at the age of one, she attended a Life, Death, and Transition workshop given by Dr. Kübler-Ross in 1982.

This encounter with Dr. Kübler-Ross inspired a lifelong association. She subsequently served as chairman of the board of directors of the Elisabeth Kübler-Ross Foundation based in Zutphen, Netherlands, and as such, helped to develop the Hospice Foundation there.

She continues to write articles, lead workshops, and lecture on the work of Dr. Kübler-Ross.

Cathleen Fanslow-Brunjes, R.N., M.A., C.N.S.

C athleen Fanslow-Brunjes is a recognized expert in the areas of death and dying, bereavement, nursing, and hospice care. A student and former colleague of Dr. Kübler-Ross, she has worked with more than 25,000 dying patients, their caregivers, and the professional staffs involved with them. She has lectured and conducted workshops throughout the United States and Canada, as well as Western Europe.

Her recently released book, *Using the Power of Hope to Cope with Dying: The Four Stages of Hope,* chronicles what the dying taught her during the past three decades.

Cathleen Fanslow-Brunjes was a pioneer in the hospice movement. She created the hospice program for New York City's Visiting Nurse Service; worked at the first certified hospice program in Long Island, New York; established the first free-standing hospice in Switzerland; and was director of nursing at Calvary Hospital, in Bronx, New York, a specialty hospital for advanced cancer patients, considered by many to be the first hospice in the U.S.

She was also the first Clinical Nurse Specialist in Oncology and Thanatology licensed in New York State and created the Standards of Care for the Terminally Ill, the protocol that is used throughout the U.S. Veterans Administration (VA) Hospital System. Cathleen Fanslow-Brunjes has received numerous honors and awards for her pioneering efforts.

Sarah Ferguson, Duchess of York

Sarah Ferguson is a spokeswoman, writer, film producer, and benefactress. She is also a prevalent public speaker for health awareness, personal development, and global charity. When effected by her own grief, the Duchess of York found in Elisabeth the perfect healing combination of compassion, comfort, and humour.

Gregg M. Furth, Ph.D.

The late Dr. Gregg Furth was a Jungian psychologist who met Dr. Kübler-Ross in 1970, maintained a close association with her throughout her life, and was a contributing author in her acclaimed book *Living with Death and Dying.*

Dr. Furth spent the last 35 years counseling emotionally disturbed and terminally ill children and adults, and working as a Jungian analyst. He conducted hundreds of workshops worldwide on hospice training, death, dying and bereavement, symbols in healing, and training in therapeutic art methods. His recent research led to the original writing on the topic of Amputee Identity Disorder, which was first published as a journal article in 1977. His book *The Secret World of Drawings: A Jungian Approach to Healing Through Art* is published in six languages. He was a graduate of The C.G. Jung Institute, Zurich, and, prior to his death, he was practicing and teaching at the Guild of Analytical Psychology & Spirituality in London, England.

Joan Halifax Roshi

Joan Halifax Roshi is a Buddhist teacher, Zen priest, anthropologist, and author. She is founder, abbot, and head teacher of Upaya Zen Center, a Buddhist monastery in Santa Fe, New Mexico. She has worked in the area of death and dying for more than 30 years and is director of the Project on Being with Dying through Upaya. She is founder and director of the Upaya Prison Project, which develops programs on meditation for prisoners.

Joan Halifax Roshi studied for a decade with Zen teacher Seung Sahn and was a teacher in the Kwan Um Zen School. She received the Lamp Transmission from Thich Nhat Hanh, a Vietnamese Buddhist monk who was nominated for a Nobel Peace Prize in 1967, and was given Inka by Roshi Bernie Glassman. A founding teacher of the Zen

Peacemaker Order, she has focused her work and practice on engaged Buddhism for more than three decades.

Stefan Haupt

Stefan Haupt is an award-winning director associated with Fontana Film GmbH in Zurich, Switzerland. His 2002 film, *Utopia Blues,* won the Swiss Film Award for Best Feature Film. *Facing Death,* the documentary on Elisabeth Kübler-Ross, M.D., was nominated in 2003 for the Swiss Film Prize of Best Documentary. The film received the Study Award from the Swiss Federal Office for Culture, and was a finalist in the 2004 International Health and Media Award, U.S.A. The film is distributed in the U.S. by First Run/Icarus Films, as well as his newest award-winning film *A Song for Argyris*.

He is currently president of FDS, the Swiss filmmakers' association, and resides in Zurich, Switzerland.

Tom Hockemeyer

Tom Hockemeyer, co-founder of the German publishing house Silberschnur Verlag, is a well-known novelist and author of books on reincarnation and the laws of karma under the pseudonym Trutz Hardo. He published German editions of five of Dr. Kübler-Ross's books and subsequently became a lifelong friend.

He studied reincarnation and past-life regression under Richard Sutphen, one of America's most famous regression therapists and teachers on reincarnation. In addition to his publishing activities, he is the most widely known group regressionist and trainer of regression therapists in Germany.

Barbara Marx Hubbard

A noted author, futurist, citizen diplomat, and international speaker, Barbara Marx Hubbard is in the forefront of an emergent, post-conventional worldview called Conscious Evolution.

She co-founded several major organizations including the World Future Society and the Association for Global New Thought. She is the host and producer of the seven-part documentary series currently in development entitled *Humanity Ascending: A New Way through Together*. This transformational series presents vital elements to awaken the codes for our own conscious evolution and offers direction, meaning, and a vision toward our birth as a new humanity.

Her books include: *The Hunger of Eve: One Woman's Odyssey Toward the Future; The Evolutionary Journey: Your Guide to a Positive Future; Revelation: Our Crisis is a Birth — An Evolutionary Interpretation of the New Testament; Conscious Evolution: Awakening the Power of our Social Potential;* and *Emergence: The Shift from Ego to Essence.*

Rick Hurst

R ick Hurst's film credits include *Steel Magnolias, M*A*S*H,* and *Anywhere But Here*. He has also had starring roles in three television series and is widely known for his role as Deputy Cletus Hogg in the TV series *The Dukes of Hazzard*.

Mwalimu Imara, D. Min.

D r. Mwalimu Imara is professor emeritus of Human Values and Ethics at Morehouse School of Medicine in Atlanta, Georgia. He is currently a faculty member of the Gestalt Center for Organizational Systems Development in Cleveland, Ohio.

A graduate of Meadville Theological School, University of Chicago, Dr. Imara worked with Dr. Kübler-Ross from the beginning of the death and dying movement at the University of Chicago Hospitals. He wrote the thematic chapter, "Dying: The Last Stage of Growth," in Dr. Kübler-Ross's book *Death: The Final Stage of Growth*.

Dr. Imara is an Episcopal priest and holds Diplomat status in the American Association of Pastoral Counselors. He lectures and conducts workshops and retreats on the topics of health and religion, meditation, bereavement, counseling the seriously ill, the spiritual foundations of counseling, and catastrophic loss.

Gerald Jampolsky, M.D.

Dr. Gerald G. "Jerry" Jampolsky is an internationally recognized authority in the fields of psychiatry, health, and education. In 1975, he was the co-founder of the original Center for Attitudinal Healing for Children and Adults with Life-threatening Illnesses in Tiburon, California.

Through his work at the center, he created the first support group model now used extensively worldwide. There are now more than 130 independent Centers for Attitudinal Healing, serving communities in 26 countries.

Dr. Jampolsky has published extensively. His books include *Love Is Letting Go of Fear, Teach Only Love: The 12 Principles of Attitudinal Healing, Goodbye to Guilt, Out of Darkness Into the Light,* and *One Person Can Make a Difference*.

He is married to Dr. Diane Cirincione, and together they have lectured and consulted worldwide on practical spirituality for nearly 25 years. They have each been the individual recipient of numerous international awards including the Jehan Sadat Peace Award and the Pan Humanitarian Award.

Melina Kanakaredes

Melina Kanakaredes is the star of the television show *CSI: New York*. She received two Emmy nominations for her recurring role as Elena Andros Cooper on the television show *The Guiding Light*. She also appeared on *NYPD Blue* and in the feature films *15 Minutes,* with Robert DeNiro and *The Long Kiss Goodnight,* with Geena Davis and Samuel L. Jackson.

A second-generation Greek-American born in Akron, Ohio, she began her career as an actress in a community theater production of *Tom Sawyer* at the age of eight. She attended Ohio State University and later graduated magna cum laude from Point Park College in Pittsburgh. After performing with the Pittsburgh Playhouse and appearing in commercials and industrial videos, Kanakaredes moved to New York and worked in off-Broadway productions.

Carol Kearns, Ph.D.

Dr. Carol Kearns retired after 25 years in private practice as a clinical psychologist in San Francisco. She specialized in crisis counseling, and has been active with The Compassionate Friends, an international organization of bereaved parents as well as other Bay Area bereaved parent organizations. She is writing a book about rebuilding her life after her daughter's death.

Amy Kuebelbeck

Amy Kuebelbeck is the author of *Waiting with Gabriel: A Story of Cherishing a Baby's Brief Life,* a poignant book, which was also published in Italy as *Aspettando Gabriel.* She is a freelance writer and former reporter and editor for The Associated Press, and has written for the *Seattle Times* and the *Los Angeles Times.* She edits an internet site for Perinatal Hospice.org, and is currently co-authoring a book about continuing a pregnancy with a terminal prenatal diagnosis, which is to be published by Johns Hopkins University Press. She is one of the millions of people who never met Dr. Kübler-Ross, yet was helped by her life and work.

Stephen Levine

Stephen Levine's bestselling books *Healing Into Life and Death, A Gradual Awakening,* and *A Year to Live* are considered classics in the field of conscious living and dying. His latest book *Breaking the Drought: Visions of Grace* is a book of poems that was published in 2007. He and Ondrea, his wife and spiritual partner, have counseled the dying and their loved ones for more than 30 years. Together they wrote the acclaimed *Embracing the Beloved* and *Who Dies?* They live a meditative life in the mountains of the American Southwest, where they created Warm Rock Tapes to distribute past productions and to share their guided meditations.

Robert T. McCall

Robert McCall first won acclaim as an aviation artist, and then gained widespread attention in the 1960s when *Life* magazine commissioned him to prepare a series of paintings on the future of space travel. A short time later he became one of a select group of artists chosen by NASA to document the U.S. Space Program. He has covered many space launches since that time. Most recently, he completed a series of five portraits of significant Arizona aviators that were commissioned by the City of Phoenix.

He developed conceptual paintings for such films as *Star Trek* and *2001: A Space Odyssey*. He also collaborated with the acclaimed writer Isaac Asimov on the book *Our World in Space*. His work is prominently displayed in the Pentagon, the Air Force Academy, the Smithsonian Air and Space Museums, as well as in many distinguished private collections.

Gladys McGarey, M.D, M.D.(H)

Dr. Gladys McGarey has been a family physician for more than 50 years. She is internationally known for her pioneering work in holistic medicine, natural birthing, and the physician-patient partnership.

Dr. McGarey is a founding member and past president of the American Holistic Medical Association, past president of the Arizona Board of Homeopathic Medical Examiners, and a member of the board of directors of the American Board of Holistic Medicine. Her work through the Gladys Taylor McGarey Medical Foundation has helped to expand the knowledge and application of holistic principles through scientific research and education. She is the author of *The Physician Within You* and *Born To Live,* and her latest book, *Living Medicine,* will be available in the spring of 2009.

Dr. McGarey has won numerous awards for her pioneering work. She recently completed a humanitarian mission in Afghanistan through the international non-profit group Future Generations to provide medical care in underserved rural areas. She was one of Dr. Kübler-Ross's physicians during the last years of her life.

Hervé Mignot, M.D.

Dr. Hervé Mignot was the force behind the palliative care movement in France and founded the Elisabeth Kübler-Ross Association in 1993. He continues as its president, and also teaches palliative care and grief support at the Universities of Paris and Tours.

Dr. Mignot is a fifth-generation physician who chose a path less travelled by his familial predecessors, all of whom become professors and academicians. He worked with Doctors of the World in war-torn and poverty-stricken areas such as Senegal, Afghanistan, South Africa, Chad, and Lebanon.

Raymond Moody, Ph.D., M.D.

D r. Raymond Moody is a world-renowned scholar and researcher, and the leading authority on the "near-death experience," a phrase he coined in the 1970s. He is the bestselling author of 12 books including *Life After Life,* which has sold over 10 million copies.

Dr. Moody continues to capture widespread public interest and generate controversy with his groundbreaking work on the near-death experience and research into the facilitating of apparitions of deceased loved ones. He is director of The Raymond Moody Research Foundation, a non-profit organization dedicated to learning, teaching, exploring, and developing techniques for understanding what happens when we die.

Balfour M. Mount, O.C., O.Q., M.D., F.R.C.S.C.

D r. Balfour Mount attended a lecture delivered by Dr. Kübler-Ross in the early 1970s on the care of the terminal patient. Following this encounter with Dr. Kübler-Ross, he found himself at a life-transforming crossroads that led him to become a pioneer in palliative care in Canada. He was the founding director of the Royal Victoria Hospital Palliative Care Service in Montreal, Canada, in 1975; Palliative Care McGill in 1990; and the McGill Programs in Integrated Whole Person Care in 1999.

Dr. Mount has authored more than 140 publications and participated in the production of 25 teaching films and audiotapes on oncology and palliative care. Since 1976 he has been chairperson of McGill's biennial International Congresses on Care of the Terminally Ill.

He is an Officer of the Order of Canada, Officer of the Order of Quebec, and recipient of the American Academy of Hospice and Palliative Medicine Lifetime Achievement Award.

Caroline Myss, Ph.D.

Dr. Caroline Myss, the internationally known medical intuitive, is also a *New York Times* bestselling author. Her books include *Anatomy of the Spirit,* which was published in 18 languages, *Why People Don't Heal and How They Can, Sacred Contracts, Invisible Acts of Power,* and *Entering the Castle.*

While Dr. Myss started as a journalist and co-founded Stillpoint Publishing in Walpole, New Hampshire, she simultaneously began her career as a medical intuitive.

In 1984, she began what became a longtime association with C. Norman Shealy, M.D., Ph.D., which would scientifically confirm her ability as a medical intuitive. As a result of the many years of successful research with her colleague, she developed the field of Energy Anatomy, and she and Dr. Shealy co-authored *The Creation of Health.*

In 2003, Oprah Winfrey offered Dr. Myss her own television program on the Oxygen network in New York, and it ran successfully for that year.

She is the leading recording artist for Sounds True, Inc., and to date has more than 180 titles in the company's library.

Elayne Reyna

Elayne Reyna, known as Bluebird Woman, is an elder of the San Juan Intertribal Council. A visionary and peacemaker, she is the founder of One Earth One People Peace Vision Inc., which is dedicated to promoting peace through the arts. Her visionary art is collected and sold internationally.

She has written and illustrated two books, *Wolf Dreamer* and *Song of the Bluebird*. She is a spiritual counselor and uses talking, dance, drum, and prayer circles to help people express grief and encourage healing through forgiveness and reconciliation.

Elayne Reyna and her many accomplishments are the subject of a chapter in the book *Real Moments,* written by Dr. Barbara De Angelis, and in *The Ways of Spirit* by Susan Averett Lee.

She and Dr. Kübler-Ross formed a sacred relationship as ceremonial sisters many years ago.

Hetty Rodenburg, M.D.

Dr. Hetty Rodenburg received her medical degree from Leyden University in Holland and went to New Zealand in 1971 to begin her medical practice. She worked as a general practice physician until 1998. During that time, she developed an interest in grief counseling; the effects of trauma on psychological, physical and spiritual health, and working with terminally ill patients, including those with cancer and HIV/AIDS.

After attending an intensive workshop with Dr. Kübler-Ross in 1988, she was asked to become a workshop facilitator. She worked and trained with Dr. Kübler-Ross and facilitated her workshops in New Zealand and other countries until 2001. She is in private practice counseling those diagnosed with life-threatening illnesses and continues to teach and facilitate seminars.

John G. Rogers, M.D.

D r. John Rogers earned his medical degree from Melbourne University in Australia, and later went on to study pediatrics. After qualifying in pediatrics, he served as a Fellow to Johns Hopkins in Baltimore, Maryland, and studied medical genetics.

Dr. Rogers returned to Melbourne, Australia, in 1976 as a medical geneticist, and was responsible for building the Clinical Genetics Unit, ultimately becoming its director. Following a diagnosis of lymphoma, he retrained as a psychotherapist with a special interest in grief and life-threatening disorders.

He was a lifelong friend of Dr. Kübler-Ross and conducted workshops for her in Australia.

Ken Ross

K en Ross is an independent commercial photographer based in Scottsdale, Arizona. He specializes in travel-location, people, and corporate photography. His work has been exhibited in the U.S., Japan, the Philippines, and Mexico.

His first book, *Real Taste of Life,* was a collaborative effort with his mother, Elisabeth Kübler-Ross. He is currently establishing the Elisabeth Kübler-Ross Foundation to further her work.

Barbara Rothweiler, Ph.D., A.B.P.P.

D r. Barbara Ross Rothweiler, the daughter of Dr. Kübler-Ross, works as a rehabilitation psychologist-neuropsychologist. She completed her doctorate at the University of Utah and postdoctoral fellowships in neuropsychology and rehabilitation psychology at the University of Washington. She has authored and co-authored papers that have appeared in professional publications, and has presented at national conferences. Her work has earned awards in teaching and research. She lives in Wisconsin with her husband and two daughters.

Sylvia and Emma Rothweiler

Sylvia, the now nine-year-old granddaughter of Elisabeth Kübler-Ross, is in fourth grade, enjoys reading, her school, her teachers and her pets. She also loves her grandmother and inherited her love of chocolate!

Emma, the now seven-year-old granddaughter of Elisabeth Kübler-Ross, is in first grade. She loves to laugh, loves her school and her teachers, enjoys learning German, and remembers special times with her grandmother.

Hope Sacharoff

Hope Sacharoff has performed on stage in New York and Illinois, including playing the role of Yenta in *Fiddler on the Roof*. Her last movie before relocating to Arizona was Woody Allen's *Bullets Over Broadway*. She has also appeared in national television commercials for such companies as Federal Express, Pontiac, and General Electric, among others.

Dame Cicely Saunders, O.M., D.B.E., F.R.C.P., F.R.C.N.

The late Dame Cicely Saunders was recognized as the founder of the international hospice movement. She utilized her training as a nurse, medical social worker, and physician to found St. Christopher's Hospice in London in 1967. It was the world's first research and teaching hospice linked with clinical care, and also was a pioneer in the field of palliative medicine.

Dame Cicely held over 25 honorary degrees and received numerous prestigious awards for her work, including the British Medical Association Gold Medal, the Templeton Prize for Progress in Religion, the Onassis Prize for Services to Humanity, The Raoul Wallenberg Humanitarian Award, and the Franklin D. Roosevelt Four Freedoms for Worship Medal.

She was made a Dame in 1980 and awarded the Order of Merit by Her Majesty The Queen in 1989, the highest personal honor the monarch can bestow and the highest award given in England.

In 2003, she was voted the third Greatest Doctor in History by *Doctor* magazine. The Cicely Saunders Foundation is a British charity formed to raise funds for an Institute that will promote high standards of clinical practice, research, and education in palliative care.

Susanne Schaup, Ph.D.

Dr. Susanne Schaup is a freelance editor, writer, and translator based in Vienna, Austria. She became acquainted with the work of Dr. Kübler-Ross when she was an editor for a publisher in Munich, Germany. In the late 1970s, she started to translate Dr. Kübler-Ross's work into German for Kreuz Verlag Publishing. In addition to her translation of Elisabeth's books, she edited two German anthologies of her own work.

Dr. Schaup also edited and translated a number of anthologies of great American classics, including the *Journals of H.D. Thoreau*. Her published works include a short monograph on Dr. Kübler-Ross for her 70th birthday, a book about children in India, a report of her own spiritual experience with cancer, and *Sophia — Aspects of the Divine Feminine*.

J. Donald Schumacher, Psy.D.

Dr. J. Donald Schumacher was named president and chief executive officer of the National Hospice and Palliative Care Organization in 2002, and president of the National Hospice Foundation the following year. He also serves as president of the Foundation for Hospices in Sub-Saharan Africa and the Alliance for Care at the End of Life.

A globally recognized authority on hospice and palliative care, he has lectured internationally on strategic planning for hospices, palliative care policy development, and clinical guidelines for HIV.

C. Norman Shealy, M.D., Ph.D.

Dr. Norman Shealy is a Harvard-trained neurosurgeon and acknowledged expert on pain and stress management. He was the founding president of the American Holistic Medical Association, and is currently President Emeritus and Professor of Energy Medicine at Holos University Graduate Seminary in Springfield, Missouri, which he also founded. A sought-after speaker and prolific author, Dr. Shealy has authored more than two dozen books, including *Life Beyond 100 — Secret of the Fountain,* and over 300 published articles.

Cheryl Shohan

Cheryl Shohan credits the years of grief and healing work she did with Elisabeth after the loss of her two children as the guiding force behind her career in healing. She is trained in grief counseling, art therapies, and intuition practice. She worked with Dr. Gerald Jampolsky at the Center for Attitudinal Healing in California for more than 30 years. She was also co-founder of the Children with AIDS Program in San Francisco, and founder and director of the award-winning Home and Hospital Program offering services for the dying in the San Francisco Bay area.

Drawing on her own experience with breast cancer, she counsels women with metastasized cancer and couples facing life-threatening diseases. She has lectured and conducted workshops throughout the U.S., Latin America, Australia, and Western Europe, including the Findhorn Foundation in Scotland.

Bernie Siegel, M.D.

Dr. Bernie Siegel, a pioneer in holistic medicine, is considered a leading expert in the art of healing. As a physician, he has cared for and counseled innumerable people whose mortality was threatened by an illness. He is a popular lecturer and the author of many bestselling books, including *Love, Medicine & Miracles; Peace, Love & Healing;* and *Help Me to Heal.* His recently published books include *Buddy's Candle* and *Love, Magic, and Mudpies: Raising Your Kids to Feel Love, Be Kind, and Make a Difference.*

Dr. Siegel embraces a philosophy of living and dying that stands at the forefront of the medical ethics and spiritual issues that face society today. In 1978, he started Exceptional Cancer Patients, a program based on "carefrontation," a safe, loving form of therapeutic confrontation. The therapy features a specific form of individual and group therapy, and utilizes patients' dreams, drawings, and images.

He is currently working on other books with the goal of humanizing medical education and medical care, as well as empowering patients and teaching survival behavior to enhance the immune system.

Robert Singleton

R obert Singleton is internationally acclaimed for his artwork featuring spiritual light. His work is represented internationally in prestigious private and public collections.

For the past 30 years, he has lived on a remote mountaintop in West Virginia where he was a neighbor and close friend of Dr. Kübler-Ross, and served as a member of her board of directors for 10 years.

In 1995, Robert Singleton founded Russell House, a sanctuary for those living with HIV/AIDS, and those who care for them.

Johanna M. Treichler, M.A.

J ohanna Treichler worked with Dr. Kübler-Ross for 10 years, teaching workshops in English- and German-speaking countries. Born in Lucerne, Switzerland, she and her husband, Ernie, emigrated to Southern California in 1966.

She received her Master's of Arts with a focus in Depth Psychology at Pacifica Graduate Institute. She is currently a Ph.D. candidate at Pacifica Graduate Institute, in Santa Barbara, California, and is writing her dissertation, *Walk Your Own Walk*.

Doreen Virtue, Ph.D.

D r. Doreen Virtue holds Ph.D., M.A., and B.A. degrees in Counseling Psychology. She is a former director of inpatient and outpatient psychiatric programs, specializing in women's and adolescents' issues. She has appeared on many national network television shows including *Oprah, Good Morning America,* and *The View* with Barbara Walters.

In 1995, she was saved by an angel during an armed car-jacking in Anaheim, California. This incredible experience was the impetus for a life devoted to researching, writing, and speaking about angels. Her most recent book, *The Miracles of Archangel Michael,* was published by Hay House in 2008.

Florence Wald, M.N., M.S., F.A.A.N.

The late Florence Wald, along with Dr. Kübler-Ross, Dr. Balfour Mount, and Dame Cicely Saunders, are credited with beginning the hospice movement. In 1958, she became dean of the nursing school at Yale. This was at a time when Yale was seeking ways in which to integrate professional schools into the university.

After hearing both Dame Cicely Saunders and Dr. Kübler-Ross lecture, her interest in end-of-life care was heightened, and she became a passionate proponent of end-of-life care. In 1971, she joined with a surgeon, a pediatrician, and a chaplain to form the first hospice facility in the U.S., located in Branford, Connecticut.

Since the 1960s, she was an advocate for patients' involvement in decision making, and an opponent of the overemphasis on technology in the treatment of cancer patients. She has published articles and book chapters on hospice care and on the role of nurses. Up until her death in 2008, she was working to establish hospice units in American prisons.

Florence Wald received numerous awards and recognition for her pioneering efforts, including induction into the National Women's Hall of Fame in 1998, being honored with the title of "Living Legend" by the American Academy of Nursing, and being named a Distinguished Woman of Connecticut. She received seven honorary doctorates from Mt. Holyoke College and Yale University.

Rita Jean Ward, O.A.M.

In 1977, Rita Ward was the first Australian to attend one of Dr. Kübler-Ross's workshops in the U.S. She visited Elisabeth again in 1981 and was asked by Dr. Kübler-Ross to become the facilitator and director of all her activity in Australia, as well as to establish the world's first Elisabeth Kübler-Ross Association.

Rita Ward's pioneering accomplishments include setting up some of the first educational resources in Australia on death and dying, grief and loss, and recovery. She trained professionals and the general public and spent many years training volunteers to work in those areas, as well as working on management committees to set up hospices to care for the dying.

In 2002, Rita Ward received The Order of Australia Medal for "Service to the community, particularly through Palliative Care Support Groups," and in 2003 was awarded The Centenary Medal for "Distinguished Service to Elderly Citizens in Providing Palliative Care."

Fern Stewart Welch

Fern Stewart Welch is a veteran writer and author of two books. She also conceived, directed, and served as executive editor on *Tea with Elisabeth*. Her other titles include the recently released *You Can Live A Balanced Life In An Unbalanced World,* and *The Heart Knows the Way — How to Follow Your Heart to a Conscious Connection with the Divine Spirit Within.*

Welch was a feature writer and columnist for newspapers in Washington and Oregon, a staff writer for First Interstate Bank of Oregon, public relations director of The Arizona Bank (now Bank of America), a freelance international travel correspondent for *The Los Angeles Times,* editorial director of *PHOENIX* magazine, and founding president of a public relations firm. She is currently a contributing editor for *One Planet Magazine* and posts a weekly InsightsOut essay on the Internet. National Public Radio recently selected six of these essays for inclusion on their online database *This I Believe*.

Marianne Williamson

Marianne Williamson is an internationally known bestselling author, television guest, popular lecturer, and spiritual teacher. Four of her books, *A Return to Love, Illuminata, Everyday Grace,* and *A Woman's Worth,* have all been number one on the *New York Times* bestseller list. Her latest book, *The Age of Miracles,* was also on the *New York Times* bestseller list.

She also edited *Imagine: What America Could Be in the 21st Century,* a compilation of essays by some of America's most visionary thinkers. She has appeared on such national television network shows as *Oprah, Larry King Live,* and *Good Morning America*. She hosts a daily *Course in Miracles* program on Oprah Radio XM 156.

Marianne Williamson also co-founded The Peace Alliance, a worldwide network of peace activists who are working together to use the power of non-violence as a positive social force.

Rose Winters

Rose Winters is a documentary film producer. Her film, *Finding Hearts at Peace,* was recently purchased for broadcast in the Middle East. She has extensive non-profit experience and currently serves on the board of the Elisabeth Kübler-Ross Foundation, as well as the For the Children Foundation, which she established to create an intentional world for children. She continues as a consultant to governmental and non-profit agencies, addressing the concerns of children and youth.

Afterword

By Karla Wheeler, Publisher

In you, gentle reader, Elisabeth has lit an eternal flame. It is the flame of selfless service to others, the flame of compassion, empathy, and pure love.

In particular, I want to honor hospice physicians, nurses, aides, social workers, counselors, and chaplains. I have witnessed your love in action hundreds of times as a hospice volunteer invited into the sacred circle of families facing the inevitable death of a dear one. Often you are called "angels" because you bring not only professional medical expertise to families served by hospice, but also an abundance of hope, support, and comfort. You fly into their lives at a time when most people flee. You shine light where society dares not look.

Because of the angels of hospice in the United States and Canada, five members of my immediate family have experienced a good death. I was privileged to be with my soulmate Gramma when she made her transition 20 years ago, and it was just as beautiful as she predicted. At that moment I knew my life's purpose: To dedicate my journalism/ publishing career to helping humanity understand that death is not the enemy, and that — thanks to hospice — no one need die alone or in pain. As the years unfolded, hospice professionals helped my father, father-in-law, and mother live their last days in peace and love, not fear. Then two years ago, when my 54-year-old husband was diagnosed with advanced cancer "out of the blue," hospice was there to support our family, especially our 14-year-old daughter. We gathered 'round his deathbed, reassuring him of our unending love and gratitude, and giving him permission to go.

The depth of my appreciation to hospice angels across North America and beyond is more profound than mere words can adequately express, for each beloved family member — until they took their last breath — lived every cherished moment knowing they were loved unconditionally.

On a professional level, hospice has enabled me to realize that no physician should ever have to say, "There is nothing more I can do for you." Rather, when it is clear that a patient's earth walk is coming to a completion, every physician can say with confidence, "There is something very important I can do for you and your family. I can have you meet with the wonderful people from hospice. They will do their best to help you live each day, each moment, free from fear and free from pain on all levels — physical, emotional, social, and spiritual." That is why 10 years ago my publishing company launched an end-of-life care newsletter for hospices to use as a tool to educate physicians about the multidisciplinary benefits of hospice care.

Yes, gentle readers, in you Elisabeth has lit an eternal flame. As you carry that torch of compassion into the lives of millions, know that you are lightworkers; you are loveworkers.

All of us at Quality of Life Publishing Company applaud you for continuing Elisabeth's groundbreaking work. We believe Elisabeth would want you to know that while the subtitle of this book reads, "Tributes to Hospice Pioneer Dr. Elisabeth Kübler-Ross," every word written on these pages truly is a celebration of your dedicated work, too.

Next time you look deeply into the soul of a patient, think of Elisabeth. Who knows? Perhaps she will be right there by your side.

How to Order

Quality of Life Publishing Co. specializes in gentle grief support and other inspirational books for readers of all ages. Here's how to order *Tea with Elisabeth* and other publications:

Bookstores: Available wherever books are sold

Online: www.QoLpublishing.com

Email: books@QoLpublishing.com

Phone: Call during regular business hours Eastern Time. Toll free in the U.S. and Canada: **1-877-513-0099** or call 1-239-513-9907

Fax: **1-239-513-0088**

Mail: **Quality of Life Publishing Co.**
P.O. Box 112050
Naples, FL 34108-1929